CONTACT WITH GOD

THE AMAZING POWER OF PRAYER

by

Jeanne Wilkerson

Edited by Brent Olsson

Harrison House
Tulsa, Oklahoma

05 04 03 02 01   10 09 08 07 06 05 04 03 02 01

Contact With God—
The Amazing Power of Prayer
ISBN 1-57794-352-X
Copyright © 2001 by Brent Olsson
Edited by Brent Olsson
P.O. Box 721396
Oklahoma City, OK 73172-1396

Published by Harrison House, Inc.
P.O. Box 35035
Tulsa, Oklahoma 74153

In loving memory of Jeanne and D.B. Wilkerson.

Thank you for leaving me
a godly heritage in which to walk.

CONTENTS

ACKNOWLEDGMENTS

I want to express my gratitude, above all, for the tireless work done by my father-in-law, James O. Sutton, Sr. Without his meticulous transcription of sermons, this project would never have come together. His extra pair of eyes was invaluable in the editing process.

My loving wife, Jene', shared in the concept of this book and helped me sort out drafts, arrange interviews, and keep organized. She is my right arm and God's precious gift to me. For her I am eternally grateful.

Billy Joe and Sharon Daugherty generously helped jump-start this project by giving me the transcripts of all the sermons my grandmother preached at Victory Christian Center. They have continued Jeanne's memory by dedicating Victory Christian Center's prayer room to her. Their support in this project has been a tremendous blessing.

Berta Bass of Kenneth Hagin Ministries has been of great assistance in providing transcripts of sermons and prophecies given by my grandmother at Brother Hagin's

School of Prayer and Healing. Berta uncovered sermons and prophecies on audiotape in her archives that were previously unreleased. I want to thank her for her selfless giving.

Many thanks to Kenneth Hagin, Sr., Freda Lindsay, and Billy Joe and Sharon Daugherty for sharing their recollections of Jeanne Wilkerson.

It has been a great pleasure to get to know Billye Brim. My family appreciates Mrs. Brim's part in keeping alive the memory of Jeanne. She has been an inspiration and help for this project.

—*Brent Olsson*

FOREWORD

Jeanne Wilkerson taught with the prophetic anointing of the last days before the coming of the Lord. It was my blessing to be a speaker with her at conferences and meetings. And I loved to sit at her feet in visits at her home, where she waited on the Lord in prayer.

I first saw Mrs. Wilkerson in Kenneth Hagin meetings in Tulsa in the late sixties. Watching her move in the power of the Holy Spirit in meetings from that time until she moved to heaven provided much of my own "schooling in the Spirit." It was electrifying.

As a usual pattern, Brother Hagin would call her up, and the Spirit upon her would lift us all to spiritual heights as she shared what she saw or spoke with an intonation of voice that matched the powerful prophetic message she delivered.

In February in the early eighties my daughters telephoned me in Helsinki, Finland, where I had returned after ministering in Soviet Russia. They told me about an annual prayer seminar they were attending and how Sister Wilkerson had seen a white horse ride into the auditorium. I prayed the meeting would extend until I could get home. It did. And I asked Mrs. Wilkerson to share the details of that special night.

She said something to this effect: "I was caught up in the Spirit when I felt someone tap me on the shoulder. It was Mrs. Hagin. She said, 'He wants you to come up and share what you are seeing.'

"I saw a rider on a white horse ride through the north wall of the building. He rode up and down the aisles. I shared that with the congregation, but I did not tell them the rider was Jesus.

"I said to the rider, 'Sir, what are you doing?'

"He said, 'I am inspecting the troops.'"

And she continued to tell me about Jesus' visit to inspect His troops, His church.

PROPHESIED FALL OF COMMUNISM

Another one of Sister Wilkerson's Holy Spirit-inspired statements comes to mind. Once we were praying with her before a trip into Communist Russia, and she prophesied, "Shortly before the coming of the Lord there will be relative freedom to preach the gospel behind the Iron Curtain. It is mercy before judgment. Work quickly while you can. The door will close again. Judgment is coming."

It was hard to believe. Jim and Kathleen Kaseman and I went regularly to KGB Russia with experienced Finnish Christians. At the Lord's instruction, we translated and published Kenneth E. Hagin's books into Russian, arranged to get them into the country, and smuggled ink to the underground press. We knew the oppressive restrictions of Communism firsthand.

But it happened just as she said. In 1989 the Berlin Wall fell, and with it the strong arm of Soviet Communism was broken. I thought of Sister Wilkerson's prophecy as we preached from the steps of the former Museum of Atheism in St. Petersburg, Russia.

TONE DOWN

Perhaps the prophetic word given through Sister Wilkerson that most affected my life is what I call the "tone-down prophecy."

CONTACT WITH GOD

My husband had been sick for a very long time, and I was so involved with his care that I really wasn't aware of what was happening in the Middle East in March and April 1986. But I was certain the Lord had told me to take a trip in April to Israel. Forty people, including servants of the Lord I've worked with from the seventies until this day, went on what we call the "tone-down trip."

I know now that in March 1986, Libya launched missiles against the United States' Sixth Fleet, which was assembled off the Libyan coast. Libya's Muammar Quaddafi ordered an attack on Americans "to cause maximum and indiscriminate casualties." On April 5, a bomb exploded in a discotheque in Berlin frequented by United States' service personnel. Of the two hundred injured, sixty-three were American soldiers. Libya was responsible.

On April 15 and 16, the United States launched a series of military air strikes against ground targets inside Libya.

On April 23, an Israeli security guard at London's Heathrow Airport discovered explosives in the false bottom of a bag that a Jordanian, recruited by Syrian intelligence, had given to his pregnant Irish girlfriend. She was to take the bag on board an El Al flight to Tel

Aviv. The Jordanian was arrested and implicated the Syrian embassy.

Saber rattling against the United States' ally, Israel, pervaded the Islamic Middle Eastern countries.

Abu Nidal, an international terrorist, vowed to take revenge on American or British tourists in Israel.

I did not know all this when Sister Wilkerson asked me to meet her at a fine restaurant in Tulsa, Oklahoma. At the end of the meal over the white, candlelit tablecloth she spoke these words: "Satan is trying to push things into happening before the time. God is sending you to say two words: *Tone down.* When you say them in the anointing and power of the Holy Spirit, they will have the same effect as when Jesus said to the storm, 'Peace, be still.' But if you say them in the flesh, then they will mean nothing."

As we moved through Israel during the last few weeks of April 1986, we saw no other tourists—even at the popular sites. We were always aware of an Israeli military presence close by. And we were aware of another One, the Holy Spirit, who accompanied us to three holy but potentially dangerous sites. A white dove was with us inside the Upper Room, inside the Dome of the Rock on the Temple Mount, and was perched in a tree above, facing us as we took communion inside the Garden Tomb.

Two Britains were shot in the walkway to the Garden Tomb a day after we were there.

My daughter, Shelli Oaks, was with me when word came to us in Jerusalem that my husband had taken a turn for the worse. We went out onto the balcony of our hotel room to pray. We had not yet been prompted to utter the words we were sent to speak, so I did not feel released to leave. As I prayed, the Lord spoke to me from a Scripture that the words were to be spoken in the north. So I continued on with the group.

When we visited Katzerin in the Golan, Lynne Hammond was amazed at the Israeli jets swooping low over our heads just before making a 90-degree turn straight upward at the Syrian border. She said, "I can see the pilots' eyes. I wish Mac could see this." Pastor Mac Hammond, her husband, had been a fighter pilot in the Vietnam War.

As we stood on the border between Israel and Syria, with two mountains bearing the electronic eyes and ears of Israel pointed toward Damascus behind us and Syria before us, we knew in our spirits this was the place. In one loud voice, the forty of us, called by God to deliver the word, shouted, "Tone down! Tone down! Tone down!"

The late April skies were unseasonably dark, and ominous clouds boiled overhead. As soon as we shouted, "Tone down!" the clouds parted and the sun broke through. Our Israeli guide was astonished.

Just after we returned to the United States on April 30, one of the members of our group heard a network news reporter say, "Sources don't really know how it happened, but the Middle East just seemed to tone down."

I saw very clearly through instances like these that Sister Wilkerson heard and followed God's voice. Her ministry indelibly marked my spirit and my own call to the Lord's service. And although she has departed from the earth, what she prophesied is still a living part of our work today.

—*Billye Brim*

INTRODUCTION

How do we really know Christianity is the truth? What sets Christianity apart from any other philosophy or creed? The distinction that sets Christianity apart and reveals its truth is that its dynamic life and power emanate from a living Jesus! There is living power behind the promises of God.

God is looking for men and women who will live out His truth and demonstrate His power to show the world He is alive and real. The Bible says, "For the eyes of the Lord run to and fro throughout the whole earth, to show Himself strong on behalf of those whose heart is loyal to Him" (2 Chron. 16:9 NKJV).

As a young boy, while listening to my grandmother, Jeanne Wilkerson, preach, I experienced the power of God to the point that my body was literally shaking. Others experienced it as well. When she would pray for people in a prayer line, for example, they would sometimes fall under the power of the Holy Spirit without her even having touched them. When my grandmother gave prophetic words by the Spirit, they always resounded with authority, always glorifying Jesus and shedding new light on the Word and will of God.

When she ministered, I saw things happen that paralleled the events recounted in the book of Acts. For example, one time while she was ministering at Victory Christian Center, the conviction of the Holy Spirit fell so strongly upon one man that he literally ran out of the service. The power of God had manifested because she prayed.

It was comforting to know that this prayer warrior was praying for *me*. I knew God was real: I saw His life lived out through her. As a teenager, I went to hear her lessons in Sunday school because they inspired me to walk with integrity before the Lord. She often said, "God didn't save you just to take your sins away. He is qualifying you for an eternal position." This temporal life has eternal consequences. I also learned through her teaching that Jesus' coming is very near.

Years have passed. I married a beautiful wife and now have two young boys. But I never forgot how my grandmother touched my life throughout my childhood and young adulthood. I knew Jesus was real and wanted to pass this same knowledge on to my boys.

INTRODUCTION

Sitting in a rocking chair one night, eagerly reading a transcript of one of my grandmother's sermons, I was gripped by the prophet Samuel's words, which she had quoted in reference to parents' praying for their children: "Moreover as for me, God forbid that I should sin against the Lord in ceasing to pray for you" (1 Sam. 12:23). When I read that, tears came to my eyes. I knew I needed to have a better prayer life. I had neglected to intercede for my family as I should have. Here was a challenge to press in deeper and to know Jesus better through prayer.

In my profession as a lawyer, I regularly plead my clients' cases in court. Now I was being summoned to the heavenly court to plead the case of my wife, children, and many others before the great Judge of the universe.

My grandmother's teaching had a way that directly but lovingly got the point across. She did not mince words but served up the meat of the gospel. Like Paul, she urged God's people to move on to maturity in Christ. (Heb. 6:1.)

The central theme of my grandmother's ministry was intercessory prayer. Prayer was the critical function of her ministry. She preferred her private prayer closet to the spotlight of public ministry. My grandmother taught that through praying in the Spirit, you can literally enter heaven's court and go before the throne of grace and know the Father God intimately. And to those who boldly approached the Master in prayer would come revelations beyond the natural man's comprehension! My grandmother said that intercession was a thrilling "safari adventure."

God wants to fulfill the great expectations you present to Him through prayer. You can learn about those great expectations God wants you to have when you openly expose your heart to the life emanating from Jesus. You will be transformed from glory to glory.

This book contains the very best of Jeanne Wilkerson's sermons on intercessory prayer. It is my hope that they will inspire you to deepen your relationship with the Lord through prayer. These messages are still important for us today because, as never before, God's people are hearing the call of the Spirit to seek the face of the Lord. He wants to open the spiritual eyes of His people to see the wonder and beauty of the grand finale He will perform in these last days.

I thank God for the spiritual heritage that my grandmother left my family and me. In preparing this book, I have felt like a miner who inherited a mine with a vein full of precious jewels. The greatest treasure anyone can have is a vibrant relationship with the Lord

Jesus Christ. What a joy it is to share with you the jewels of my grandmother's teaching of God's Word!

As you read this book, realize the inestimable value of the spiritual heritage you will leave to your family by genuinely living out your Christian life before them. You will affect future generations by the intercession you offer today.

—*Brent Olsson*

CHAPTER ONE

WHY WE MUST PRAY

I always said that no one would ever be able to take me out of the world of music because it was my life. I *loved* to sing and dance! But when Jesus found me, He changed everything. He made me a new creature in Christ. But I still get to do a little singing and dancing. I thank God today that when I have a song in my heart, He still opens the stops once in a while and allows me to sing. The only difference is now I'm singing in the Spirit.

Becoming a Christian is the greatest thing that has ever happened to me. So many things have become alive to me that I didn't understand before. For example, when I was in the world, I used to think prayer was a boring subject. I thought people only prayed when they were in

1

trouble or when they wanted to do something nice for someone. But that is just not true.

For example, have you ever noticed that when you mention the topic of prayer in most churches, people think, *Oh, how drab! How fun can praying be?* Well, let me tell you, it can be *fun!* I count it the highest privilege and honor of my life to give myself to intercessory prayer after becoming a Christian.

I have been a Christian for fifty years, and in all of my Christian life, there have never been more exciting times than those I spent seeking God. Hallelujah!

Twenty-four years after becoming a Christian, God called me to go into intercession. The Lord saw that emergency hours were coming upon the earth, and He needed intercessors. God often calls me to pray during hours of crises in the world in which He needs intercessors to stand in the gap and build up a hedge of protection where there is none.

In short, I answered the call of God to intercede. Oh, yes, I prayed a lot before I answered that call, but I had never known what intercession really was all about until God began to teach me.

Before I answered the call to intercede, I prayed "parroted" prayers. For example, when I heard somebody say a prayer that sounded good, I simply repeated it, as a parrot might have done. And I prayed that way for a while until I finally said, "Lord, I'm tired of being a parrot. I want to be fed by the Master's hand." Boy, was I surprised to find out what happened next.

God led my prayer group and me into a spiritual battle that I would never have conceived to be possible. For example, God told my prayer group that we would cross international datelines in prayer. I didn't even know we could do this! I thought, *Oh, God, how will I cross an international dateline down in the basement of a church?* It wasn't long before we got the answer.

God told our prayer group we would cross international datelines by praying Christian satellite television into existence. Back then, we didn't even know what a satellite was. You see, we began our prayer group in 1961—before we knew about satellites. Nevertheless, we just believed God and fought the good fight of faith, and sure enough, later that same year we saw Christian television introduced.

God told us many such things—secret things that enlightened us. I wouldn't trade those experiences for anything in the world. In fact, some of those special times we spent in prayer rival even the best church services I had been in before and have been in since. I just love those quiet times with the Lord! I'm not a celebrity. I just love basement prayer meetings! Hallelujah!

So, my sense of protocol is not always up to par. I'm not a big shot. I haven't been to Washington to see the president yet, but by faith I *have* entered into the presence of the King of kings and basked in His presence. And one day I'll stand before God almighty in heaven, and I think my spiritual protocol will pass when I arrive then. Hallelujah!

INTERCESSION RECONCILES GOD TO MAN

Intercession is not strange. Despite what some people may think, it isn't outlandish. Intercession is simply bringing two beings together who are separated by differences.

God illustrated this "bringing together" in His Word: God and man were once separated by sin. Therefore, it was necessary for One who knew both parties to bring the two back together into harmony and relationship. As you know, Jesus performed this function.

In the same way, intercessory prayer reconciles God to man. Intercession is the prayer by which one reconciles two parties. When an intercessor prays, he or she brings two parties who are separated by differences back together again. But intercession isn't a formula.

Do you know why the Gospel writers did not discuss Christ's prayer life in detail? Have you ever wondered why we don't even know much about how Jesus prayed? The answer is that God didn't want any of us to cut out a mold and say, "If you don't do it this way, you're not doing it right." In other words, there is not just one correct way to pray.

The act of prayer is as unique, intricate, and beautiful as God Himself. Hallelujah! Therefore, it is wrong to tell people that if they don't pray like you do, they're not praying correctly. That is simply not true!

If the universal church of the living God focused all the tributaries of prayer that flow from the main stream of God into the world today, we could turn the world right side up in no time. That is the truth! There is unfathomable power in prayer.

I sense that we Christians today have never yet realized the power at our command through prayer. Through the powerful release of prayer, for example, we can influence the world's system and bring to pass the multitudinous promises and blessings of God!

For every promise, there must be a day of fulfillment. It isn't enough to keep *talking* about the promise. We must *see* the promise come to pass!

Do you know why we need to pray? It used to always bother me when Christians talked so much about prayer. I thought, *Why do we talk about prayer all the time? What's the necessity of prayer? Why is prayer so important? And why are we commanded to pray, being assured of its blessings and benefits? Why? There has to be a reason.*

God showed me why, and I'll tell you. The reason we are commanded to maintain a vital prayer life is so that we can commune with God. When He created man in the beginning, He put him in that perfect paradise known as the Garden of Eden. It was there in the cool of the day God Himself came to earth to walk and talk with man face to face. (Gen. 3:8.) Unfortunately, the vision barrier caused by sin prevents mankind from seeing God. But God has never ceased speaking. When the Holy Spirit of the living God was poured out on the Day of Pentecost, He began to remove the sound barrier so man could hear His voice.

Likewise, because of sin, our eyes are incapable of seeing God. Consequently, we can no longer meet with Him face to face as we once could before sin entered in.

Now, we must come back into communion with God, talking and walking with Him through the new birth and by the Holy Spirit. Until the day comes again when faith will become sight and we can again walk and talk with God face to face, we must commune with God by faith. In the meantime, the only avenue of seeing Him, hearing Him, and touching Him is by moving with Him in prayer. Hallelujah!

We know that God speaks to us through His Word. He will tell us His plan and purpose for our lives as we pray to Him. When we enter into His divine presence, we learn to fellowship with Him and know Him as He really is. We will see Him in prayer, for it is only by the Holy Spirit that we can enter into His presence.

The flesh is shut out from the presence of God. But by the Spirit of the living God, we can commune with God. The minute we enter into prayer, we enter into His presence. The more we learn and do to perfect our spiritual lives, the more we will see God as He really is.

Whereas Adam once saw God with the natural eye, we can see God with the eye of the spirit through prayer. And one of these days, we shall again see Him with the natural eye. Our new glorified bodies will have that capability. Hallelujah!

Until then, we must commune with God through our spirits. We must talk to Him in the Spirit. We must learn to move with Him in the Spirit. This is the reason prayer is so necessary.

If you want to see God-fellowship and commune with Him, to learn and gain counsel from Him, you must sit at His feet, as Mary did in the New Testament. She chose the better part, which would never be taken away. (Luke 10:39-42.)

So, when you choose to sit at Jesus' feet and learn of Him, you have chosen the better part of servitude, which will never be taken away. Therefore, take some time to serve God in your prayer life. If you truly desire to hear God's voice and commune with Him in prayer, you will hear His voice.

NEGLECT OF PRAYER: A GREAT SIN OF THE CHURCH

Daniel 9:10-13 illustrates how the failure to pray was one of Israel's major sins. Likewise today, insufficient prayer is also a major sin of the church. Look at what the Bible says about this sin in the book of Daniel:

> **Neither have we obeyed the voice of the Lord our God, to walk in his laws, which he set before us by his servants the prophets. Yea, all Israel have transgressed thy law, even by departing, that they might not obey thy voice; therefore the curse is poured upon us, and the oath that is written in the law of Moses the servant of God, because we have sinned against him.**
>
> **And he hath confirmed his words, which he spake against us, and against our judges that judged us, by bringing upon us a great evil: for under the whole heaven hath not begin done as hath been done upon Jerusalem. As it is written in the Law of Moses, all this evil is come upon us: yet made we not our prayer before the Lord our God, that we might turn from our iniquities, and understand thy truth.**
>
> **Daniel 9:10-13**

The prophet Samuel, who was a great intercessor, knew that failing to intercede for others was a sin. He said, "As for me, God forbid that I should sin against the Lord in ceasing to pray for you" (1 Sam. 12:23).

Israel's neglect of their prayer lives was a sin. God gave them promises, promises, and more promises to make them the head and not the tail. He promised that they would never be defeated before their enemies and that He would always visit them and bring them out of calamity. God promised Israel victory in every battle, as long as they were obedient, dependent on Him, and willing to call upon Him in trouble.

Israel had all the promises necessary to be successful, and yet an evil empire (Babylon) captured the nation. This happened because, as Daniel noted, the people of Israel did not obey the Word of the Lord, nor did they call on Him so that He might save their nation. (Dan. 9:10,11.)

So you see, just having information isn't enough. Things that are born of God must be inspired by the Spirit and *followed up on with action.* Hearing an excellent sermon isn't enough. The world has heard preaching, preaching, and more preaching and yet is still not redeemed. Don't misunderstand me: Preaching and teaching of the Word of God is good, but after hearing, one must follow up with action. Actions must back up words, and each of us must make godly decisions after the preaching has gone forth.

Many nations are now without even a witness in their lands. A witness is necessary to spread the gospel. The Bible tells of Ezekiel who was a witness, a prophet taken into captivity of the Babylonians. A group of Hebrews had been previously taken into Babylon's captivity. God told Ezekiel the reasons for Israel's captivity. Look at what He said:

> **And I sought for a man among them, that should make up the hedge, and stand in the gap before me for the land, that I should not destroy it: but I found none. Therefore have I poured out mine indignation upon them; I have consumed them with the fire of my wrath: their own way have I recompensed upon their heads, saith the Lord God.**
>
> **Ezekiel 22:30,31**

God found no intercessors among them, and Israel went into captivity.

Intercessory prayer is so important because it comes from the heart. Prayers from the heart are sincere. God records the prayers that come from the hearts of His people. (Ps. 56:8.) The book of Psalms, the prayer book and hymnal of the Bible, is filled with prayers from the hearts of God's people. It is not a book that came from the heads of the writers. It is a book that came by the inspiration of the Holy Spirit in the hearts of God's people.

THE POWER OF THE INTERCESSOR AGAINST JUDGMENT

In the book of Exodus, Israel had seen God move in amazing and miraculous ways, and yet they still did not believe. Therefore, God said He would destroy them because of their backsliding and the hardness of their hearts. But the prayers of God's man, Moses, intervened: "Therefore he said that he would destroy them, had not Moses his chosen stood before him in the breach, to turn away his wrath, lest he should destroy them" (Ps. 106:23).

God even said to Moses once, "Moses, move out of the way; step aside," because He wanted to punish the people for their sins. (Ex. 32:7-10.) And, in fact, He would have, if Moses had not been there to intercede on the people's behalf. (vv. 11-14; Ps. 106:23.) Judgment cannot come as long as there are intercessors standing in the gap, making up the hedge between God and man.

Satan always wants the church to step aside, cease her prayers, and surrender her authority. Satan knows that if the church prays, she will continue to be the tower that stands against him. He knows that none of God's blessings can flow from heaven to earth unless intercessors are praying.

If that sounds too far-fetched for you to believe, just read your Bible. There you will find the power of an intercessor. Look at the passage in Numbers that describes the return of the twelve spies to the children of Israel. In their report of the Promised Land, the majority of the spies said that it would be impossible to go in and take the land. As you know, this lack of faith spread and led the nation of Israel into a state of rebellion against God.

> **And the Lord said unto Moses, How long will this people provoke me? and how long will it be ere they believe me, for all the signs which I have skewed among them? I will smite them with the pestilence, and disinherit them, and will make of thee a greater nation and mightier than they.**
>
> **Numbers 14:11,12**

God told Moses, "I'll just get rid of these people. I'll move them out of the way, raise you up, and let you lead a nation that is greater than these." Yet Moses continued to intercede for the children of Israel. In his answer to God, Moses foreshadowed Christ as a mediator between God and man. Moses pled, "Pardon,

I beseech thee, the iniquity of this people according unto the greatness of thy mercy" (v. 19).

We can see from Moses' example that intercessors are never self-centered when they pray. They do not think of themselves. We can see an example of this selflessness in the life of Jesus. Jesus did not think of Himself. He thought of His responsibility and the reward awaiting Him—and us—for His coming to earth and fulfilling the Father's will. He gave Himself to save His people. Intercession invokes God's great saving power, and it can save many lost souls. Moses was zealous, not for himself, but for God. Look again at what he did. He reminded God of His name and His promises.

> **And Moses said unto the Lord, Then the Egyptians shall hear it, (for thou broughtest up this people in thy might from among them;) and they will tell it to the inhabitants of this land: for they have heard that thou Lord art among this people, that thou Lord art seen face to face, and that thy cloud standeth over them, and that thou goest before them, by day time in a pillar of a cloud, and in a pillar of fire by night.**
>
> **Now if thou shalt kill all this people as one man, then the nations which have heard the fame of thee will speak, saying, Because the**

Lord was not able to bring this people into the land which he sware unto them, therefore he hath slain them in the wilderness.

And now, I beseech thee, let the power of my Lord be great, according as thou hast spoken, saying, The Lord is longsuffering, and of great mercy, forgiving iniquity and transgression, and by no means clearing the guilty, visiting the iniquity of the fathers upon the children unto the third and fourth generation.

Numbers 14:13-18

As you can see, the intercessor will always remind God of His long-suffering and mercy. Hallelujah!

I don't care what kind of sins people have committed! Don't join forces with the enemy and say, "It is too late. They ought to get it together on their own." Moses could have said that about the children of Israel. But instead of speaking negative words about the situation, he stepped into the gap between God and man to form a hedge of protection, saying, "God, don't let the enemy gain the victory in this situation. We have told them who You are and what You have done. Now, Lord, remember Your long-suffering and Your mercy."

Moses continued his intercession in this way:

> **Pardon, I beseech thee, the iniquity of this people according unto the greatness of thy mercy, and as thou hast forgiven this people, from Egypt even until now.**
>
> **Numbers 14:19**

Those who know their God can have a say in things that happen on this earth. That is the truth. They can! How do I know this? Because God listened to Moses instead of destroying the children of Israel. He granted Moses' request, saying, "I have pardoned according to thy word" (Num. 14:20).

The Lord continued His promise:

> **But as truly as I live, all the earth shall be filled with the glory of the Lord. Because all those men which have seen my glory, and my miracles, which I did in Egypt and in the wilderness, and have tempted me now these ten times, and have not hearkened to my voice; surely they shall not see the land which I sware unto their fathers, neither shall any of them that provoked me see it: but my servant Caleb, because he had another spirit with him, and hath followed me fully, him will I bring into the land whereinto he went; and his seed shall possess it.**
>
> **Numbers 14:21-24**

As you can see, although the disbelieving children of Israel were punished, they were not destroyed. That is because Moses stood in the gap as an intercessor for them, and God demonstrated His mercy.

PARENTS STAND IN THE GAP FOR THEIR CHILDREN

The Bible shows us a family promise that Christian parents should not ignore: "For the promise [of the gift of the Holy Spirit] is unto you, and to your children, and to all that are afar off, even as many as the Lord our God shall call" (Acts 2:39). Furthermore, the Bible says, "Believe on the Lord Jesus Christ, and thou shalt be saved, and thy house" (Acts 16:31).

These verses contain vital information that you can't afford to forget. Promises of God's blessings are given to you *and* your family. They will be fulfilled as you walk in obedience to God's Word and stand in the power of prayer.

If you will seek His face, God says, "I will not only bless you, but your children will inherit every blessing that you have." (Gen. 28:4.) The blessings of God are for you and your children—every one of them. Hallelujah!

As parents you have not only the right, but also the command from God to stand in the gap, interceding for your children until the promises of God are brought about in their lives.

We are seeing youth come to God as never before, and that is wonderful! But many of the youth coming to God have parents who don't even serve Him. It should be the other way around! God says, "A good man leaveth an inheritance to his children's children" (Prov. 13:22). In other words, the children should not lay up blessings for the parents, but the parents should lay them up for the children.

Any time children have a need, *the parents* are the ones who should be their intercessors in the presence of the Master. Parents are to stand by the power of the Holy Spirit as mediators between heaven and earth, between God and their children, until the children are standing with God on their own.

For example, look at the life of Job. He was one of the great intercessors of the Old Testament. The Bible says that he made intercession for his children "continually." (Job 1:5.) Job's prayer life should serve as an example to parents today. First Timothy 5:8 says, "But if any provide not for his own, and specially for those of his own house, he hath denied the faith, and is worse than an infidel."

Providing prayer for family members is a parent's greatest responsibility. Parents should pray for the needs of their family members as consistently as they provide for their material needs.

INTERCESSORS SEE GOD'S PLAN

Sometimes people ask me, "What do you do spending all that time in prayer?" Well, I usually tell them I come into the presence of God, and then Jesus unveils to me the glory of oncoming visitations-things He will do and plans He will fulfill in the future.

I have seen God's plans come to pass in the natural, earthly realm. But I get even more excited when God gives me glimpses of things in the spirit. When that happens, I just stand back in awe to see how His plans will come to be.

It is in the spirit that you can foresee the plans of God. Time doesn't drag on in the spirit realm. If it did, eternity would be boring, but it won't be. In heaven, we will do things with more beauty, precision, and purpose than we have ever experienced on this earth. However,

God wants to give us a taste of that in this life. He wants to show us the skill, the art, the beauty, the majesty, the glory, and the power of life in God. When we live in this way, heaven is demonstrated here on earth.

It is up to us as intercessors to become so saturated with heaven that we bring it down to earth. Heaven isn't just a place—it is a nature and way of life. It is a character trait, a lifestyle, and a quality of being. Heaven contains a power and performance that those on earth don't know anything about.

I used to wonder why people didn't get excited about going to heaven. Now I know why. One lady said to me, "I think heaven is just a place where we'll sit around on clouds and strum on harps."

I said, "Well, I don't want to go there!" Who would want that?

In the Bible Jesus described heaven the only way He could to those who haven't been there. He did that because our natural minds have limitations. He could only take things that we understand in the natural to make comparisons.

One example of such a comparison is Jesus' description of heaven as a city. (Matt. 5:35.) That means all the country folks will want to experience the city of heaven! They'll want to see the lights and tall buildings.

And once they have seen all the activities, people, performances, great inventions, and the power and glory of heaven, they'll never want to go back to the country!

Our God is not a God of monotony. He is a God of diversity. He doesn't do the same thing the same way every time. He is the God of many voices! He is the God of many attributes! He is the God of many abilities! He is the God of grace! And He is such a tremendous force for righteousness that nothing can withstand Him.

One night in our intercessory prayer meeting, the Spirit of the Lord fell upon us. The Lord began to reveal His plan in such a beautiful and colorful description. He began to unveil to us through prophetic utterances that before Christ died, heaven and earth could not truly benefit from all of God's goodness. The relationship God wanted the whole earth to enjoy was not fully possible because of the enmity between God and man that sin had created. The two sides could not enjoy peaceful relations before Jesus Christ came to earth. Jesus didn't die only to save mankind; He died to reestablish a peaceful relationship between heaven and earth. Hallelujah!

During that same prayer meeting, the Holy Spirit began to reveal to us the great period in which we would rule and reign with Jesus; we will even experience interplanetary travel in the heavens! For thirty to forty minutes, the Spirit of the living God spoke in technical terms about the beauty of things that our natural minds could not know. Praise God for His revelation knowledge!

Revelation knowledge must be spiritually discerned. You would not try to render a description of a great musical composition to a deaf man, for he could not hear it. It would be impossible to describe the beautiful revelation knowledge present at that prayer meeting to someone who is spiritually blind and deaf. He would not be able to understand. Only those who have been made alive in the Spirit and whose senses know God and the spirit world can see and hear into the spiritual realm. Only the spiritually alive person can discern between the natural and spiritual worlds.

Jesus said, "Blessed are they which do hunger and thirst after righteousness: for they shall be filled" (Matt. 5:6). Hunger and thirst come when you seek God to such an extent that the Creator of the universe Himself indwells you and endues you with His own divine life. When that happens, the world will have to admit, "You have been with Jesus." It cannot be hidden! The fact that you have been communing with Jesus can be heard in your voice, seen in your eyes, felt in your touch. When you lay your hands on people, they won't feel your natural hands, but the compassionate hands of Jesus Himself.

THE RAIN AND THE FIRE OF GOD'S SPIRIT

Have you ever noticed what the leaves on a tree do? They soak up water from the atmosphere and provide life-giving oxygen back to the earth. Well, tree leaves are much like God's children. In the Bible, we are likened unto trees planted by rivers of water, except our leaves will never fade because we have been planted next to the living water of the Holy Spirit. (Ps. 1:3.) As a leaf on a tree can draw from its source of water and gather moisture from the surrounding atmosphere, so can the Christian gather from God's supply of His own life-giving Spirit.

In addition, natural leaves give off moisture as vapor, which is released back into the clouds. The clouds in turn pour rain back upon the dry earth, and the cycle continues. This is exactly how God intended for us to be. As we pray, our intercession is released into the spiritual clouds of heaven, which then pour out the rain of His Spirit into the earth. This remarkable principle works according to the amount of spiritual moisture we draw from the atmosphere of the Spirit of life. In turn, we again give out spiritual life to the world around us through our prayers.

Another symbol the Bible uses to describe the Holy Spirit is fire. Hebrews 12:29 says, "For our God is a consuming fire." When the Spirit of God falls, He brings the fire of the Holy Spirit. (Acts 2:3.) As you know, fire can set wood ablaze as well as cause water to boil. When we see the mighty sweep of God's eternal presence once again, we'll see lives become ablaze with the glory of God.

First Kings 8 describes an occasion in which King Solomon led Israel in seeking the Lord, and God's glory fell like a cloud of smoke: "The cloud filled the house of the Lord, so that the priests could not stand to minister because of the cloud" (vv. 10,11). But notice that the glory came from God, not from Solomon. The fire of the Holy Spirit is not something we can work up. It is something that must come from our own spirits, where the Holy Spirit dwells. Fire falls as a result of the Spirit that dwells within us, and once it is ignited, it can move with divine power to break the shackles of spiritual bondage.

MAKE PRAYER "PRIME TIME" IN YOUR LIFE

We should be persistent in prayer. In Luke 18, Jesus taught this principle through a parable, an illustration by which His followers could learn a heavenly truth.

> **And he spake a parable unto them to this end, that men ought always to pray, and not to faint; saying, There was in a city a judge, which feared not God, neither regarded man: And there was a widow in that city; and she came unto him, saying, Avenge me of mine adversary. And he would not for a while: but afterward he said within himself, Though I fear not God, nor regard man; Yet because this widow troubleth me, I will avenge her, lest by her continual coming she weary me. And the Lord said, Hear what the unjust judge saith. And shall not God avenge his own elect, which cry day and night unto him, though he bear long with them? I tell you that he will avenge them speedily. Nevertheless when the Son of man cometh, shall he find faith on the earth?**
>
> **Luke 18:1-8**

This parable illustrates the kind of faith and prayer that will not take no for an answer. When you know that God promises to provide for your needs and that Satan can't do anything to stop Him, then you will receive your answer. But you must not turn back or give up until this happens.

Jesus calls this kind of persistence in faith "importunity."[1] (Luke 11:8.) Importunity is refusing to give up or to lose heart.[2] In researching the meaning of the word "importunity," I found that it is akin to what we think of when something is "prime time" on television. And, as we know, prime time is when the greatest viewing audience tunes in to a particular program. The networks are suggested to air the best they have to offer in "prime time." Well, in the same way, we must have "prime time" prayer with God. We must give our prime time to the greatest listening audience anyone could ever have—God.

Prayer changes us. The Word says that as Jesus prayed, His countenance changed into the image of glory:

> **And it came to pass about an eight days after, these sayings, he took Peter and John and James, and went up into a mountain to pray. And as he prayed, the fashion of his countenance was altered, and his raiment was white and glistering.**
>
> **Luke 9:28,29**

Do you want to be changed like that when you pray? Then learn how to enter into God's divine presence by the power of the Holy Spirit.

God said, "I know your works, that you are neither cold nor hot. I could wish you were cold or hot" (Rev. 3:15 NKJV). We already know what heat does to water: it boils it. In much the same way, the Holy Spirit "heats up," or inflames, the spirits of men and women with passion, first for God and then for seeing His name vindicated in the earth among mankind.

Jesus began His earthly ministry with prayer, and He closed it with prayer. At the height of His ministry, He prayed with strong emotion, even tears. (Luke 22:41-44.) He was a man who was totally dependent on His heavenly Father to provide Him with the power necessary to fulfill God's will in the earth and to defeat the powers of the enemy.

But even before Jesus began His earthly ministry, God raised up intercessors to spiritually pave the way for Jesus' ministry. One such true intercessor is Rachel of the Old Testament. She said, "Give me children, or else I die" (Gen. 30:1). The heart of an intercessor wants to birth life. Well, Rachel's miraculous ability to bear children symbolized her bringing forth life into the world, foreseeing the signs, wonders, miracles, glory, and power of Jesus Christ.

Rachel was bold with God. Esther, another woman of the Old Testament, was bold as well. She went unbidden into the presence of her husband, the king, risking her life. (Est. 5:1.) But a decree of death had been issued against her people, and going to see the king was more important to her than her own life. She responded to the situation by saying, "Fast ye for me, and neither eat nor drink three days, night or day: I also and my maidens will fast likewise; and so will I go in unto the king, which is not according to the law: and if I perish, I perish" (Est. 4:16).

So, into the presence of the king she went unannounced, risking her life to do so. But the king had mercy on her and asked, "What wilt thou, queen Esther? and what is thy request? it shall be even given thee to the half of the kingdom" (Est. 5.3).

It was then that Esther "importuned" the king for the freedom of her people, the Jews, whose lives and bloodline had been threatened. As I said, the word "importunity" in the Bible would mean "prime time" in today's language. So we could say that Esther made a prime-time appointment with the king.

In the same way, prayer should be prime time in our own lives. And if it is, we will enjoy the greatest, most powerful listening audience in the universe—the King of kings and Lord of lords. Praise the name of Jesus!

ENTER GOD'S PRESENCE BY PRAYING IN THE SPIRIT

By fulfilling our commitment to consistent and frequent prayer, we learn how to enter into God's presence. It is in times of prayer that the Holy Spirit ushers us into the presence of the King of kings. Prayer draws us into the very throne room of God, for in the Spirit, there is no distance. Prayer crosses all time barriers, all geographical boundaries, and takes you directly into the presence of God.

The Bible talks about "groaning" in the spirit. (Rom. 8:26.) This "groaning" in the spirit is "God talk." (1 Cor. 14:2.) In other words, those groanings are mysteries, which the Spirit prays through you. This is "God talk." When you speak with groanings in the Holy Spirit, you are expressing something that is too deep to be said with mere words. So, God, the Holy Spirit, does the speaking for you. That is the reason we need an interpreter to understand someone else's prophetic tongue. In this way, the Holy Spirit communicates both with us and through us. What a beautiful combination!

Let the Spirit speak for you. He alone knows how to address God from His high station. In and of myself, I would be at a loss in the presence of the King of kings, but the Holy Spirit is totally at home there. He escorts me into God's presence, and I can boldly enter in by the blood of Jesus. (Heb. 10:19.) Once I'm in my Father's presence, He always asks me, *What is your request?*

You see, when you're in the spirit, your heavenly
Father sees and hears you; you have His full attention.
Of course, God can see and hear you all the time in the
natural, but when you're in the spirit, it is as though you
are actually in His throne room. Your physical body is
still on earth, but your spirit perceives God in heaven.
Learn to visualize this type of communion with God.
Picture Him with His Father's heart welcoming you
home into His presence and longing to meet your
needs, to teach you what you need to know and to
show you things to come.

By communing with God this way, we will begin to
see signs and wonders occurring in our lives. Great
visitations of grace shall come to us when we give
ourselves to intercessory prayer. We won't have to beg
for great signs and wonders. Rather, they will visit us
frequently. They will follow us just as a loyal pet follows
its master. Signs and wonders followed Jesus during His
earthly ministry, and they will follow us too, as we pray.

God wants to lift the sound and wisdom barrier in
your life. He gave me a word that describes His heart
and how He longs to share good gifts with His children:

The Spirit is saying, *I have many things that I want to
reveal unto you. I have much wisdom laid up for the last
days. In the treasure chambers of the temple (which is*

the storehouse of God) there is much wisdom; there is much knowledge in store. But you have not come; you have not asked. Therefore, My storehouses are full, and I am wanting to give out these great treasures.

I have much that I am longing to unveil and show you in many realms of the time and life on earth yet to come. I have many places I want to take you. I have many days of power that I want to share with you. But your eyes are still too clouded, too taken up with the things of time and the five senses. The Spirit is having difficulty getting through to you. It grieves My heart.

The time warrants that, of necessity, I call many of you out into certain areas now, to ask and challenge you to surrender yourself that I might shed this wisdom and knowledge. I am wanting to give light concerning the activities for nations. There is much knowledge of the glory of God that I'm longing to shine upon you. I want to stagger you again, not with unbelief, but with My glory. I want you to hear My voice. I want you to know that I am ready to move, to show, to reveal, to illuminate, to teach you wisdom, and to teach your hands how to make war. I want to instruct you how to go out effectively against the enemy in this hour, so that you will not come back in defeat time and time and time again. I am crying out to you: lift up your voice like a trumpet, and I will show you my salvation! It is ready to be revealed in the last days as men have never seen yet.

Prayer is an ongoing process, not just a one-time thing to do. Prayer is the lifestyle and practice of holding on to the things of God and letting those things of God hold on to us until, through us, Jesus can operate in the earth as He did when He was here in the flesh.

Therefore, be diligent to pray, always believing that you're not only performing mighty works for the kingdom of God, but you're also getting to know and communing with God. That is what prayer is all about: getting to know your heavenly Father.

CHAPTER ONE

LIFE WITH OR WITHOUT PRAYER

Time and again throughout the Old Testament, the nation of Israel fell into the sin of unbelief. But there was something else, another sin, that helped to create this condition: *a lack of prayer.*

Likewise, the lack of prayer has been a sin of the church for a long time. It hasn't always been this way, however. The Bible describes the early church turning their world upside down with their prayers. (Acts 17:6.) Had the church remained strong in prayer until this present day, we would be performing the same feats the early church did and watching God move in incredible ways.

The early church knew how to move cities and even nations for the kingdom of God, but through the years, the power of those miracles has diminished. Somewhere along the way, the church began to take the gospel for granted, failing to act on it in faith and thus missing many of the blessings God had for her.

DON'T TAKE THE GOSPEL FOR GRANTED

It is important to never take this glorious gospel for granted! You may think that you will always have the bright light of God's Word available to you, but darker days are coming. You can't just sit in the seat of ease in Zion after you have been saved and filled with the Holy Spirit. You must maintain your spiritual life and keep yourself sharp in the Word. You must allow the same source that produced that life—the Holy Spirit—to sustain it.

The gospel can be compared to light. It is like the moving of the sun, which rises on one horizon, crosses the heavens, and sets in another horizon. While we have the sunlight, the gospel, it is day. But the Bible says the night is coming, and unless we continue to walk in the light, the darkness will overtake us. (John 12:35.)

According to Romans 15:19, Paul took the gospel to a place known as Illyricum. After he did, the churches and people were so blessed by the beautiful light of the glorious gospel that signs and wonders followed.

Today that same region is known as Albania. It is the place where Paul performed so many signs and wonders in the name of Jesus, and the glorious gospel was proclaimed with all of its beauty and power. Through Paul, the people of Albania saw the gospel manifested through powerful signs and wonders.

But notice the more recent history of this nation where so many miracles had been performed. Albania is the first nation in the world to declare herself totally atheistic. Today it is a communist nation, and most of the people are Muslims. In 1967, after a fiery speech by Albania's ruler, two thousand convents, monasteries, mosques, and churches were taken over to be put to use for "better purposes."[1] The ministers and priests were assigned to hard labor, and since 1967, the practice of Christianity has been totally forbidden. Bibles were collected and burned, and even the mere possession of a Bible warrants one's being shot by a firing squad.

It is hard to believe this is the same place that once saw such mighty signs and wonders!

A broadcast from the capital city of Tarana reported
that severe measures had to be taken to erase Christianity
from the minds of the people—extreme measures such
as sealing Christians in barrels and rolling them alive
into the sea.[2] The bishop of Duress in Albania was
enclosed in an iron cage the size of his body. Inside, the
walls were covered with spikes that penetrated his flesh.
He was then pushed along the streets until he died.[3]
The London Daily Telegraph reported that several
priests had been shot by firing squads.[4]

Children are placed in state nurseries from birth.
Their parents are not allowed to have custody of them.
They are given two hours visitation privileges daily to
spend with the child, if both the child and mother desire
it.[5] Over half the population in Albania is under twenty-
five years of age.[6] Less than five percent of its citizens
are ever permitted to leave the country.[7] Albania is the
second smallest country in Europe, the size of Belgium.
It is bordered by Yugoslavia, Greece, the Adriatic, and
Ionion Seas. It is Europe's most primitive, backward
nation, though the Communist party's chief objective is
to create a "new man."[8]

This place that had actually witnessed the birth of the
gospel and had seen the signs and wonders of our God
within its borders is no longer walking in His blessings.
Sadly, if in our own lives we don't take advantage of

God's hour of visitation, as in the case of Albania, we will not always enjoy divine demonstrations from God.

Freedom is the most valuable commodity in the world. People who travel to the underprivileged nations of the world will often tell you what a privilege it is to enjoy religious freedom in America. For example, a friend of mine who traveled to preach at a church in a communist nation told me about the adversity he witnessed. He said that the Christians in that country spend hours upon hours crying out to God to give them just a few hours of freedom to preach the gospel.

THE WORD IS FRUITLESS WITHOUT PRAYER

I want to tell you that the neglect of prayer is one of the greatest sins of the church today, especially here in America. You may say, "Oh, the church has all it needs in the Word." But the Word will fall to the ground, fruitless, without prayer.

You can rattle off Scriptures all day long, but if you don't apply the Word in your life through obedience, then that Word can't accomplish what it is sent to do. Deuteronomy 28:38 tells us that if the Israelites did not obey the Lord, even though they may have taken much seed from the land of their captors, they would receive only a small return on it. Obedience is the key, and one area in which many Christians have been disobedient is the priority they place upon prayer in their lives.

The Word of God has been broadcast by radio, television, and word of mouth to millions and millions of people. But not all of those people have been saved, healed, and delivered. That tells us that if the Word could accomplish mighty works on its own, then we would see many more nations of the world on their knees before God. The problem is that the people who do hear God's Word lack the obedience in their prayer lives to make it work. That is why there is so little return on all the Word that goes out into the earth.

It is for this reason that my heart is so stirred for the nations of the world. I have stayed up until the wee hours of the morning to pray for the current state of Albania, especially after I realized how Paul had taken the gospel there with signs and wonders following. I have cried to the Father, "My God, my God! Here is a church that had been filled with Your Spirit for so long and yet is so far from God today." They lost their boldness in prayer, and their freedom followed.

COME BOLDLY INTO GOD'S PRESENCE

The Bible says that we are to approach God boldly through our prayers: "Let us therefore come boldly unto the throne of grace, that we may obtain mercy, and find grace to help in time of need" (Heb. 4:16). Jesus, our High Priest, has gone into God's presence to give us access to the Father. (Heb. 4:14.)

The Old Testament describes God's coming down to Mount Sinai, where His presence appeared as smoke at the top. The people were told not to come too close, not to gaze upon God's presence, and not to cross the line separating the people from God. Only those ordained by God were allowed into His presence.

Only about seventy out of the whole multitude were able to go up that mountain where the presence of God dwelled. (Ex. 19.)

After the Mount Sinai experience, the tabernacle was set up in the wilderness. The only place the masses of people could enter was the outer court, in order to bring their sacrifices to the priest. Only those who were ordained, or chosen, by God—the priests of the Levitical order of Aaron—could go any farther into the Holy Place. (Ex. 28:29.) Furthermore, only once a year, one man, covered by the blood of a sacrifice, could enter the Holy of Holies where the Shekinah glory of God abided. (Lev. 16:1-6.)

People in the Old Testament had to follow these rituals because sin had separated them from God. Because of God's holiness, they could not approach Him in their sin-stricken state. Sadly, this condition remained throughout the Old Testament. The men and women under this old covenant anticipated the hope of their salvation and waited all their lives to see the Messiah. Most never did.

When the time had come, Jesus came to earth to redeem mankind, and He overcame sin by giving Himself as a sacrifice. He went into the presence of the Father on mankind's behalf. There, He opened the way for every blood-washed child of God to come into the Father's presence on his or her own. God made this way available through the new birth and through prayer.

What a privilege that is! It is a privilege we should never take for granted.

In the Old Testament, the priest was the one who went into the presence of God on behalf of the people. Today God speaks to His people directly through His Word and the prophetic voice of His leaders.

Therefore, if you're a believer today, you are a priest with access into the very presence of the living God. You don't have to be kept out of God's presence as the people of the Old Testament were. Praise God! Today God bids you to "come boldly unto the throne of grace" (Heb. 4:16).

Jesus has gone into the presence of God and opened the heavenly doors that were once closed for us. He actually opened the heavens for the first time when He was baptized in the river Jordan and the Holy Spirit descended upon Him like a dove. (Luke 3:21,22.) The heavens opened—never to close again! Hallelujah!

Jesus has gone back to heaven and is now seated there on what is known as the throne of grace—not *one of* the thrones of grace—but the *only* throne of grace. (Heb. 4:16.)

It is through Jesus that we have access to the mercy, grace, power, dominion, and authority of the living God! And the good news is that by prayer, we can go into the throne room of grace any time that we have a need!

Does the church have needs today? Are individual members of the church in need? Of course. Many Christians have settled into a pattern of being lukewarm. That is why believers must go into the presence of God as priests and intercede for the church.

THE GREAT SERVICE AND BLESSING OF INTERCESSION

Intercession takes discipline, and it requires self-sacrifice. As an intercessor, you have to give selflessly out of what you have.

Today when someone applies for a job, usually the first thing they want to know is what the benefits are. They may also ask, "What are the hours? How long of a vacation will I get?" Rarely does an applicant ask, "What services can I offer you?" Instead, it is almost always about the benefits that person can gain for himself. It is human nature to ask, "What will *I* get out of this?"

The beauty of intercession is that it is the greatest opportunity for service one will ever have to give *unto others*. When given out of a heart of service to God, it yields even greater benefits because the intercessor reaps what he or she sows! The Bible says, "He which soweth bountifully shall reap also bountifully" (2 Cor. 9:6). It also says, "They that sow in tears shall reap in joy" (Ps. 126:5). That is the law of seedtime and harvest.

Again, the Word says to come boldly before God. (Heb. 4:16.) What does that mean? How are you to "come boldly" to the throne of God? First, you must come with reverence and respect for who God is. He is the King of kings and Lord of lords. However, if you go in prayer to the throne of God often enough, there is a familiarity that comes from spending time with Him. You will get to know Him well, even to the point that you will understand His mind, His will, His purposes, and His pleasure. But even though this understanding will come, never forget that God is the awesome Creator of the universe, and He deserves all honor, glory, and praise.

Have you ever known some people who defer to others who seem to be more important (as though there were any person among us who is more important than another)? Well, that is how you should approach the throne room of God. You must defer to God because of His importance.

I did not understand all of this when I was younger, but after nineteen years of interceding and spending time in God's presence, I learned!

People used to say to me, "What do you do all day in prayer? You poor thing to have to pray all the time."

Do I seem like a "poor thing"? Does it seem as though I don't have sense enough to find anything else to do? Well, let me tell you, I *do* have sense to know what to do and how to best spend my time. And I'll tell you that during my times of intercession, I am paid the greatest royalty one could ever be paid.

I come to sit at Jesus' feet like Mary of old who chose the better part, which would never be taken away. (Luke 10:42.) She chose to sit at His feet and learn of Him.

You don't really know the Word until you sit at the feet of Jesus, who is the true Word. (John 1:1.) He has taught me and given me light on Scriptures I never understood before. He has shown me things to come in great, video-like prophecies of God. We may call them "visions," but they are actually nothing but the video screens of God flashing upon the eyes of our spirits— plans that He intends to fulfill and bring to pass at a later time.

God will show us where future events will happen and how they will come to pass. It is exciting! I have gotten to the point where I would rather be in intercession than in some church services which seem a little dull by comparison! Don't misunderstand me. We should go to church, but sometimes we just sit there and look at each other, acting proper and religious because we think we should.

One time I thought to myself, *My dear, what would they do if I moved out into the workings of the Holy Spirit?* It would probably scare many of them to death! But perhaps they need to be scared to begin to understand and experience some of the things of God.

It is time that we become bold in our faith. I had never realized the importance of coming *boldly* before the throne of grace until I had prayed for a gentleman for many months. He had been healed from cancer five times, but the sixth time that the cancer reoccurred, he died. After his death, I became very upset. So I went to the Master and said, "Lord, You have to explain this to me. I don't understand why this man died. I know we believed in faith for his healing."

Well, God didn't respond to me instantly. But one night as I prepared for bed, closing the day with the Word and praying in the Spirit as I always did, God answered me. All of a sudden, I was taken in the Spirit up to heaven, where I saw both Jesus and this man who had died. In the vision the man came over to me and spoke. Now, I knew his voice. Even though he was in heaven, I recognized him.

He said to me, "Jeanne, your prayers were not lost. The Lord is allowing me to show you something by the Spirit. You are well known here because of all your prayers. You appear here often."

THERE ARE NO DEAD SAINTS

Wasn't that good of God to show me that vision? You see, there are no dead saints. When the body dies, the spirit and the true person are more alive than they ever were before.

God has also taught me that in the church, two groups of people dwell in God's presence. There are those in heaven dwelling in His presence, and there are those on earth who live in His presence. Though we are still on earth and they are absent from us now, we all come together in the Spirit when we on earth partake of communion in memory of the Lord's death. Through prayer, we come into God's presence. The only difference between them and us is that the people who have passed on stand on one side of the communion table, whereas we stand on the other. But actually, they are more alive than they were when they walked with us on earth! There aren't any dead saints.

You see, sometimes we are somewhat ignorant concerning the operation and workings of our spiritual lives after death. Such ignorance can breed fear. But we don't need to be frightened by that life on the highest plane of existence. It has vistas of unlimited beauty with knowledge and wisdom that we could not possibly fathom in this earth.

Because of this, God is teaching us to become accustomed to the spirit realm. He wants to acclimate us so that we are more comfortable with that realm than with this one. The Bible says that there was no way that hell or earth could hold Jesus after He was glorified. He *had* to rise again—He just automatically came up! (Acts 2:24; Eph. 1:20.)

Before the day of the Rapture comes, you need to begin to automatically gravitate toward the spirit realm because at the time of the Rapture, you will be drawn by the irresistible power of the living God. It will so captivate you—so magnetize you—that you won't be able to hold yourself back. And this former life will look like absolute rubbish in comparison!

A VISION OF THE MARRIAGE SUPPER

One night God allowed me to see a vision of the marriage supper of the Lamb. I want to share it with you because it will help you see what I'm talking about.

Sometimes we get the idea that heaven will look like outer space does, with ethereal blobs floating around everywhere. But that is *not* what heaven is like. Heaven is even more real and more concrete than this world.

In my vision, heaven was the most beautiful setting you can ever imagine. It reminded me of a coronation of a king or queen—or the marriage of Lady Diana and Prince Charles. The marriage supper of the Lamb had all the adornments of a significant and beautiful ceremony. But even our most extravagant ceremonies on earth cannot compare to the marriage supper of the Lamb.

You ask, "Will we be able to eat there?" Yes, we will eat, if we want to. With our glorified bodies, we will have the capability of eating or not eating as we please. We will not need to eat food to exist, but we can enjoy it as we desire to.

In the vision God gave me, I saw the most glorious fountain. It was more beautiful than anything you'd see on earth.

You see, everything in heaven has a theme that has been copied on the earth. For example, the table for the marriage supper was set up to be in the shape of the cross. One table was longer, stretching farther than one could see. Then, there were two other tables that branched out from the central one, completing the shape of the cross.

Everything with God is orderly. For example, here on earth the armies of Israel didn't break rank even when they were in battle. In fact, their secret that caused them to be so victorious in battle was to use a certain formation. Battle strategists today who have gone back to investigate the secrets of the Israelites' strategy found something very interesting. The formation of Israel's troops consisted of one long center column with two columns branching out from the central one. In other words, they always marched in the formation of the cross.

Therefore, when God looked down from the heights of heaven, He saw the Israelites in the formation of the cross. Of course, this foreshadowed the death of His Son, Jesus Christ, when He would forever conquer our greatest enemy, the devil. I'm sure that whenever God saw His troops marching in this formation, He would say, "I honor those troops, and I will fight with them." And it worked. Israel would win their battles!

GET TO KNOW GOD THROUGH PRAYER

God is a good God. I learn so many things when I sit at His feet. I am able to come boldly into His presence. Because God is on my side, I am able to deal with adverse circumstances, unforeseen events, godless people, and evil situations sent from the enemy. I know God so well that I know He will honor my prayers.

Do you know Him that well? Do you know that He will back you up because He believes in you as much as you believe in Him? This happens when you become a true man or woman of prayer. He will say of you, as He said of Abraham, "I know him" (Gen. 18:19).

How is God able to know us? He knows us when we become familiar with Him in the spirit—when we talk to Him often, when we commune with Him. He gets to know each of us just like a good friend.

Do you know what the word *communion* means? It means to share something in common with someone.[9] When you commune with God through the Holy Spirit, you become lifted up to the level of His Son, who can speak to God on His own level.

When we study the Scriptures, we find that the primary cause of all failure is a lack of prayer. It began in the Garden of Eden when Adam and Eve were tempted to take their eyes off of the Tree of Life and instead looked to the Tree of the Knowledge of Good and Evil. There is no record in the Scripture of their ever consulting or communing with God about this, and Adam and Eve missed the mark, falling far short of the glory God wanted to reveal in them. If they had overcome that temptation, God would have taken them on to another level, another test to prove their faithfulness to Him. Then, had they passed each of those tests presented before them and kept their eyes on the Tree of Life, listening to God's Word and His voice as He came in the cool of the day to walk and talk with them, they would have gone on to overcome the outside forces of sin and Satan. They would have gone on to eat of the Tree of Life, which would have given them immortality, and they would have never died.

That was God's intention. But because of their lack of prayer, or communion, with the Father during this test, they fell short of the marvelous glory that God wanted to reveal through them.

But thank God for redemption! Jesus Christ came to reverse the situation. Christ was the second Adam; He was tempted at every point just as Adam was, yet without sin. (Rom. 5:14,15; Heb. 4:15.) Therefore, He earned the privilege of attaining the glory God wanted to reveal in mankind.

PRAYER: A TRANSFORMING EXPERIENCE

Have you ever noticed that many of the great experiences of prayer in the Bible took place on mountaintops? The greater your experience and knowledge of God becomes through your communion in prayer, the higher the spiritual elevation God will raise you to. Your relationship with God is progressive, continually ascending to higher heights.

Jesus went to pray on top of Mount Herman, which is 13,000 feet above sea level, the highest point in Israel. When Jesus prayed there, the two worlds, heaven and earth, met. There, Elijah and Moses appeared to Jesus, Peter, James, and John. (Matt. 17:1-9.) The world that had been invisible to them became more real than the one that was visible.

The reason we can't often see into the world of the spirit is that sin has blinded our eyes. It has erected a sight and sound barrier between us and the spiritual realm. God has always been speaking to us, but before we were born again, we lacked the Spirit of the living God on the inside of our beings to notice His voice.

But on Mount Herman, God revealed Himself. God gave Peter, James, and John a preview of the great translation to come, when all believers will be changed in a moment of time just as Jesus was changed. (1 Cor. 15:52.) The disciples no longer saw Jesus just as a man in the flesh but as a glorious light with deity shining through Him. This is only a type of what the church will undergo at the Rapture.

Throughout the years as I have prayed, God has spoken to me many times, but one thing He has told me stands out. He told me the hour would come in the history of the church when the brilliance of Christ would shine out from certain individuals so greatly that those who saw it would not even notice the people themselves. Instead, they would see the glorious light of God. Hallelujah!

You see, Adam and Eve failed to pray enough to escape temptation, and as a result, they brought the greatest catastrophe upon the human race. Later on in the Bible, Abraham couldn't wait for the fulfillment of God's promise of a son. He wanted to make it happen by himself. But the Bible says, "They that *wait upon the Lord* shall renew their strength; they shall mount up with wings as eagles; they shall run, and not be weary; and they shall walk, and not faint" (Isa. 40:31).

Just because something doesn't come to pass immediately doesn't mean you should give up your faith. The Bible says, "If thou faint in the day of adversity, thy strength is small" (Prov. 24:10). We must hold on to God's promises tightly until they come to pass!

There is no record that Abraham prayed before he took Hagar the Egyptian and brought forth a son, Ishmael, with her. (Gen. 16:1-16.) Prayer could have stopped Abraham from making this mistake, which is still causing problems in the world to this day.

If you can learn from these men of old and begin to pray before you act, you won't have messes like "Ishmael-problem children" to clean up. You will escape problems in churches, in relationships, and in the workplace that many other people experience.

Prayer really works! When I think about that, I get fired up with the Word of God. I may not always quote it, but I do fill myself up with it and wait for the Holy Spirit to bring it up on the inside of me. Then, believe me, I'm fired up to act! The Bible says, "But the Comforter, which is the Holy Ghost, whom the Father will send in my name, he shall teach you all things, and bring all things to your remembrance, whatsoever I have said unto you" (John 14:26). That is the job of the Holy Spirit. My job is to fill my vessel with the Word—reading it, applying myself to it, and then praying it by speaking it forth. Then I look to God and listen to what the Holy

Spirit is saying to me about the situation. He will quote the Word to you.

PRAYER: AN INCENSE BEFORE GOD

In Exodus 30, God gives us a beautiful analogy between prayer and the pure gold in the Old Testament temple of God. According to the Scriptures, the altar was the highest piece of furniture in the tabernacle. It was overlaid with *pure* gold, not with inferior gold like all the other pieces of furniture were made.

When you minister at the altar of God, you are ministering in the presence of the Lord Himself. In the Old Testament, the priests burned many pounds of incense on the altar before the Lord. This incense is a type, or shadow, of prayer. In Psalm 141:2 David said, "Let my prayer be set before thee as incense."

God instructed the priests of the Old Testament to burn so much incense upon the altar that all odor of the flesh was eradicated. God wants the fruit of His people's work to give off a pleasant scent. God is a God of fragrance. He is very sensitive to odors, and He wants His people to smell "perfumed" in the spirit.

The book of Proverbs describes different women in various states of spiritual cleanliness. One of them is the odious woman. (Prov. 30:23.) She was a woman who was so full of the works of the flesh that she became repugnant before God. What she really needed was a good cleansing in the spirit.

I asked God one time, "Lord, did You have a sanitation department in the Old Testament?"

Oh, yes, He said. *And I still have a sanitation department. One of these days I will come to the door of My church's sanctuary with a sanitation truck, and I will clean the place out until My people won't even recognize the place for its cleanliness.*

God doesn't necessarily like all the things His children do that they like to call "works of the spirit," when actually they are no more than works of the flesh. That is why God outlined His divine sanitation program in the book of Exodus. He called His children to burn the incense morning and evening at His altar to cleanse themselves.

All of this represents something that God is trying to show us. The incense is a type of prayer that comes before the very presence of God. God is saying through this type and shadow, *I do not want to pick up any odor of the flesh in My sanctuary at all. I want none of it—no*

*remembrance of those fleshly works coming before Me. I
want your righteousness to be solely based on the work
of My Son, Jesus Christ.*

The priests of the Old Testament were told to
maintain the altar of God. In the outer court was the
brazen altar, on which they performed the sacrifice and
spilled the blood of the animal. Then they took a coal
from the altar and went into the Holy Place, putting it
there on the golden altar of incense, the tallest piece of
furniture in the temple.

The priest was to maintain the burning of the
incense at all times. The Lord said to Israel, "Don't ever
let the fire on this golden altar of incense go out." (Ex.
30:8.) The incense ascended to the nostrils of God
constantly—a beautiful type of prayer without ceasing.

You may not be aware that all the time you are
praying, your prayers are ascending like incense before
God's throne. The fact that Scripture says to pray
without ceasing may worry you (1 Thess. 5:7), but it
shouldn't. You may ask, "How can I do that? There are
other things I have to do. I can't pray twenty-four hours
a day!" Well, you don't do it all yourself. This Scripture
is referring to the church, the body of Christ. She is told
to not cease in prayer.

You see, if prayer in the church dies off until the embers of this glorious fire go out, then God will write the word *Ichabod* over our doors and say, *the glory has departed.* (1 Sam. 4:21.) That is why the message of prayer must be brought to the church. This fire is never to go out—the church is to pray without ceasing. And the design of the Levitical priesthood shows how this operates.

THE PRIESTLY MINISTRY OF THE BELIEVER

As a believer, you should know how God ordained the priesthood in the Old Testament and then for the early church in the New Testament. It was first established for the Jewish people. Therefore, we Gentiles have a hard time understanding it sometimes, because we don't know everything about the Law of Moses. You see, the Levitical priests were called to duty by a divine appointment.

Believers should be "on call" today. If the church were operating as she should—with every one filled with the Spirit and hearing God's voice—the Holy Spirit could select a member from the body to pray for someone else and eliminate that person's need to call others for help. The believer-priest would get his assignment to pray from God.

The body of Christ should be a universal intercession network. The Holy Spirit knows when there is a need in the body of Christ, and He wants to meet it. The Holy Spirit speaks to the one He knows will pray it through. The "SOS" He gets from the intercessor goes directly into the presence of God. The distress call sets heaven into operation, and the Holy Spirit goes to work on the problem.

So, you see, an intercessor is to pray because of a divine call on his or her life. The Holy Spirit will answer the call of the believer who is filled with Him. That is how it ought to operate.

The reason it doesn't always work and we don't always get the answers we need is that we're faulty in our operation. The whole body of Christ should be filled with the light and life of Jesus Christ.

As New Testament priests, we're supposed to minister on behalf of others. First John 5:14 says we can have confidence when we stand in the ministry of a priest through prayer: "And this is the confidence that we have in him, that, if we ask any thing according to his will, he heareth us." Remember, the Word says to come boldly into God's presence. (Heb. 4:16.)

Therefore, if we know God hears us when we pray, we know that we have the petition we have asked for.

That is the ministry of a true priest—to be one who knows how to pray.

The Bible says, "If any man see his brother sin a sin which is not unto death, he shall ask, and he shall give him life for them that sin not unto death. There is a sin unto death: I do not say that he shall pray for it" (1 John 5:16). All unrighteousness is sin, but some sin does not necessarily lead to death. Now, there is a sin unto death, and Jesus does not say that the believer should pray for someone who has committed it. However, the believer-priest who sees his brother committing a sin that is not unto death is chosen of God to come boldly to the throne of grace and request life for that brother.

You have to know the God in whom you have believed. You cannot presumptuously or irreverently enter the presence of God. You must go in with confidence in the Holy Spirit.

The believer-priest is to be a maintainer of life in the body of Christ. He is to be a minister of the life of God. And if he sees a brother growing cold and drifting away from the things of God, he should not look just at the sin, but also at God, who has promised life.

I used to have some relatives who did many things they shouldn't have done. For example, they drank and partied a great deal. They had actually been born again and filled with the Holy Spirit at one time, but they had fallen back into sin.

That tried my faith. Yet when I went into God's presence over this and sought Him for many years, God said to me, *Satan will kick up all the dust he can, but when the dust finally settles, I'll fill them again with my Spirit, making them living examples because of your intercession.* God even went on to tell me about the ministry one of them would have. God showed me that He would fulfill the call on this person's life. And He did.

You see, without prayer, not much will happen. For example, the two men in the Scriptures who committed spiritual suicide were men who never prayed. They were Saul, the first king of Israel, and Judas, the man who carried the moneybag for Jesus and traveled with Him for three and one-half years. There is no record in the Scriptures that either of these men had a prayer life. Consequently, they committed spiritual suicide.

The hour in which we're living today will force us to make many important decisions. The church, too, will have to make these decisions as the Holy Spirit begins to call. In these last days, intercession is going forth and God is raising up people to pray as I have never seen in the last twenty-five years. Let the Holy Spirit show you how to pray. Let Him flow through you. He is an expert, and He is skilled in the art of petitioning the Father.

THE GREAT INTERCESSORS OF THE BIBLE

I have studied the lives of Noah, Daniel, and Job, teaching for one year on them and their accomplishments. These are three great intercessors of the Old Testament. God also commended Samuel, who continued to pray for Saul until God convinced him not to because He had rejected him. (1 Sam. 15:35; 16:1.)

When God sees that He can no longer reach an individual, He may say to you, *I don't want to waste your ability to pray for him—don't pray for him any longer.* God is a God of conservation, not of waste. He will never let your prayers go to waste. He will never call you to prayer for a situation, a church, or a people He has already written off.

On the other hand, when God speaks well of people, you can know He is truly pleased with them. He doesn't just speak His praises randomly. Therefore, you should strive to be sure that your record of prayer is a good one. Ask yourself, *What mark would appear beside my*

*name in God's books? What would God have to say
about me?*

In Ezekiel, God says, "Son of man, when the land
sinneth against me by trespassing grievously, then will I
stretch out mine hand upon it, and will break the staff of
the bread thereof, and will send famine upon it, and will
cut off man and beast from it: though these three men,
Noah, Daniel, and Job, were in it, they should deliver
but their own souls by their righteousness, saith the Lord
God" (Ezek. 14:13,14). God is a just God, and He would
stretch out His hand against any people who persistently
sinned against Him.

I spent nineteen years praying for a certain church
because God showed me a vision for that church that
you wouldn't believe. When I began praying for it, He
said, *This church is like Lazarus—it is sick unto death.*
(John 11.) *But don't sit down like those who came to the
cross and just sat down and watched My Son, Jesus, die.*
(Mark 15:29-32.) Then God told me He was raising up
intercessors in the church, just as He raised up Lazarus
from the dead. (John 11:43,44.)

God told me, *If you will go into intercession, then I
will show you the things I intend to do for this place.*
Well, I went into intercession for this church and stayed
in it every night for six years.

After that, God let me go back to public ministry, but I still prayed for that church three nights a week. Several years later, God let me go further into public ministry, and I backed that church up in prayer only two nights a week.

Nineteen years went by like this. Finally, God showed me an amazing vision for this church. I saw cancers removed and heaped up in a pile. I saw crutches stacked all over the place. I saw a majestic eagle with a long wingspan, representing the government of God, in that place. I saw the eagle slay a serpent that was hindering the work of God in that place. Afterward, I saw it fly over and land on the seat behind me. The Spirit said, *Command this eagle, and it will do your bidding.*

As I spoke what I saw God wanted it to do in the Spirit, the eagle would fly to certain places. It had such telescopic vision that it could see from a great distance. It could also pick up the scent of a serpent, and I saw it leave its perch and fly down one of the aisles after a long black serpent. The eagle swooped down with its talons to pick up that serpent and squeeze the life out of it.

Through the years, I saw the fire of God sweep through that church as I prayed for them. With my spiritual eyes, I actually saw Jesus Christ walk the aisles.

Every step He took on the floor burst into flames with
the power of the living God as He passed. I saw miracles
come to pass in that church that God had foreseen years
before. I saw people in cars coming from everywhere to
be a part of this.

When God first showed me this vision of the church,
He said, *I can't get through to them. I have come down
to look at the situation in this church to see if it is up to
My standard.*

Then I saw two angels walk into the church, carrying
a measuring stick in their hands. They said they were
sent there to measure the spiritual standard of that
place. They were there to pronounce judgment.

Now, before we started to pray for them, that church
was not up to God's standard at all. However, after we
started to pray, God told us these angels could not pass
judgment as long as the intercessors were in that place.

Unfortunately, one day some key leaders in the
church took a stand against the intercessors. When I
heard this, I wept and thought, *Surely they don't mean
this.* But they wouldn't rescind their position. So I went
to the church to pray one night and asked God what I
should do.

In all the forty-seven years I attended that church,
God told me to submit to whatever happened. But this

time when I went to Him, He said, *You're not going to stay there. You're leaving that church.*

He told me the spiritual light in that church would grow so dim that if people weren't careful, it would go completely out. So I left.

When I left the church, I did hold a business meeting in which I announced that God had dismissed me. I spoke of the beautiful vision God had for that church, and I told the people that I wasn't the only one who had seen these visions. Many other ministers who had come there had prophesied the same things. Nevertheless, the moment I walked out of the building, they closed the intercessory prayer groups.

I had been gone from there for over two years before the Lord told me that the place that received me next would receive the blessing of all the years of intercession that the former church could have had but turned down. After feeling like a misplaced person, I finally asked God, "Where do I go?"

Not surprisingly, He told me to join myself to the very place I didn't want to! I walked into a certain church one Sunday morning, and God said, *You are to join yourself to this chariot for a season. I will use you here.*

Do you know what happened? I saw the things in my vision for the other church happen in this new church.

God even blotted out of my memory the forty-seven years of fighting for and desiring above everything else to see His blessing on the former church. It seemed as though I had never even been there.

Now, getting back to the three great intercessors, Ezekiel says, "Even if these three men, Noah, Daniel, and Job, were in it, they would deliver only themselves by their righteousness" (Ezek. 14:14 NKJV). The good news is that the intercessors would at least be able to save themselves. Even if the people for whom you are praying do not allow God to work in them, your prayers are not a loss. God will still deliver you.

Intercessors are beloved people. Heaven calls Daniel "greatly beloved" three times in the Bible. The first time is when Gabriel came to him.

> **Whiles I was speaking in prayer, even the man Gabriel, whom I had seen in the vision at the beginning, being caused to fly swiftly, touched me about the time of the evening oblation. And he informed me, and talked with me, and said, O Daniel, I am now come forth to give thee skill and understanding. At the beginning of thy supplications the commandment came forth, and I am come to skew thee; for thou art greatly beloved.**
>
> **Daniel 9:21-23**

The only thing his enemies could find against Daniel was that he prayed too much. Therefore, the only way they could find to ensnare him was to pass a law forbidding prayer.

We see in Daniel 9:23 that God called Daniel "greatly beloved." Daniel 10:18 also records God's use of this term of affection: "Then there came again and touched me one like the appearance of a man, and he strengthened me. And said, O man greatly beloved, fear not."

Gabriel went on to tell Daniel some marvelous things. This wasn't just an emotional outflow of God. God is not moved by emotion and sentiment as we are. He doesn't just say things to coddle or flatter people or to gain advantage, as human beings often do.

Daniel was an avid student of the Word. He knew his people did not match up with what the Word said about them. He knew that the condition of captivity and bondage his people were in was not the will of God for them.

Since Daniel knew this was not the will of God, he began to read the prophecies of Jeremiah, which said they were only to be in captivity seventy years. (Jer. 25:11,12; 29:10.) Sixty-eight years had passed when Daniel discovered this truth (Jer. 28:3,11), and although Israel was still in bondage, he saw that the time for freedom was close at hand.

But when Daniel realized this, he didn't just say, "Praise God, it is spoken in the Word, and it will come to pass on its own." No, it wouldn't! Before the captivity could be broken, the prince of the powers of the air had to be dealt with in the heavenlies through prayer.

In Daniel 9:2 it says, "In the first year of his reign I Daniel understood by books the number of the years, whereof the word of the Lord came to Jeremiah the prophet, that he would accomplish seventy years in the desolations of Jerusalem." Daniel had studied the Word, but it wasn't enough to set Israel free.

The same is true for us today. It isn't enough for us to have enlightening Bible studies and understand the will of God and His promises. We can't just say, "Bless God, I'll just confess the Word and everything will be fine." No, it won't! We have to do something to act on that confession. The promise must be birthed through prayer.

Daniel set himself to do something. He *prayed.* Daniel said, "And I set my face unto the Lord God, to seek by prayer and supplications, with fasting, and sackcloth, and ashes" (Dan. 9:3). He wasn't even guilty; his people were. But he identified himself with the sin of his people. That is what the Spirit of Christ does.

You should identify with your church in intercession. You should confess their failures and shortcomings. But never forget to come back to plead God's promises of mercy as you come boldly to the throne of grace.

THE GOSPEL WAS MEANT TO TRAVEL

Although the early church was born in the Middle East, it was not the will of God for the gospel to remain static and stay there; it was meant to travel throughout the world. Like the sun, God meant for the gospel to travel from east to west. When it was time for the gospel to move west, God moved a group of women to pray by the riverside in Europe. They set themselves to pray daily according to the will and purpose of God. When they prayed to God to send the gospel to Europe, God sent Paul.

The Holy Spirit intervened in Paul's mission and turned him back from going east. He told Paul that He had heard the cries of a group of women on a riverbank in Europe. (Acts 16:6-14.) Because of their prayers, they received a visitation from God.

If you want an answer from God, ask Him to show you the direction in which He is moving and then follow that direction.

Begin to pray forcefully against the powers of hell that would attempt to hinder you. Pretty soon, you will notice a difference in your prayers. Say to yourself, as Daniel did, "I will not quit until this captivity is broken and my people are set free!"

If we had enough people in the church today with hearts to pray in that manner, we could save America! In Ephesians, we see what the New Testament says about intercession:

> **Finally, my brethren, be strong in the Lord, and in the power of his might. Put on the whole armour of God, that ye may be able to stand against the wiles of the devil. For we wrestle not against flesh and blood, but against principalities, against powers, against the rulers of the darkness of this world, against spiritual wickedness in high places.**
>
> **Ephesians 6:10-12**

When this verse says "high places," it means places of authority.

I have been to Washington, D.C., and I have seen the capital of our nation and the ruling seat of our government. Let me tell you, that is the place toward which U.S. citizens need to direct their prayers. If they don't, our nation will miss the plan of God. The world system will never save

America. It is the church that is going to have the power to turn the tide and save America.

PRAYER: ONE OF GOD'S GREATEST WEAPONS

Did you know that you can even extend time by prayer? Hezekiah did it in the Old Testament. The prophet Isaiah told Hezekiah that his life was coming to an end, and so he turned his face to the wall and prayed. He hadn't even finished praying before God heard him and sent Isaiah to say, "I have heard your prayer and seen your tears, and so I will extend your life. You will live an additional fifteen years." (Isa. 38:1-5.)

God showed our prayer group that in the years we interceded for our nation, we were holding back God's judgments on America. Well, if we can hold back judgment on America through our prayers, we can also hold it back for members of our families. Even churches would be judged if it weren't for intercession. If Satan could get God's intercessors to stop praying for the church, he would make sure judgment would fall, including death, diseases, and scourges we have never seen.

But intercessors are holding judgment back. Praise God! Through prayer, we can extend time. We can anoint ministries. We can release finances. Prayer is one of the most powerful forces in the universe.

God told our prayer group that prayer is one of the greatest weapons in His arsenal. But so often it has been ignored; nobody had come to call for it.

Well, it is time we call for it! We must call for the power of prayer to be released into this world. We must be aware of our current needs, just as Daniel knew of his own generation's needs.

Did you know the Jews kept such detailed records that they knew exactly when—to the day—the Messiah, Jesus Christ, would arrive on the earth? Well, now it is time to look for His return. We must read the signs of the times, keeping accurate records and flowing with the moves of the Holy Spirit. We must pray to understand the times and seasons of God, so we can perform mighty signs and wonders in Jesus' name.

Let me share with you a prophecy the Lord gave me about increasing our spiritual senses:

> *Awake, O church of God. Put on your beautiful garments of light and life. Get the shoes on your feet because there will be music in this great celebration! There will be dancing in My house as when the*

prodigal returned. There will be a celebration like you have never seen before. Your eyes cannot yet fathom it, and you cannot yet believe what your ears are hearing.

If only now you were not so dull spiritually, the Holy Spirit would unveil to you things that are beyond human comprehension. When you have grown just a little more, I will draw back the curtain on some beautiful things—things that are coming onto the scene from God, things the church will enter into. But first, I had to arouse you and awaken you and cause you to stand at spiritual attention for you to hear again what My Spirit wants to speak to you.

I have things to say unto you; I'm longing to visit you with great visitations. I will be seen again in your midst as John saw Me on the Isle of Patmos when he was in the Spirit on the Lord's Day. He was caught away in My presence. And one of these days there will be such a drawing up of the people of God by the magnitude of My presence that you will literally see Me. I will appear to you.

Praise God! Let us look for that great move of God, but let us not look passively. It is time to act! It is time for us to come together in prayer to perform mighty works on the earth. It is time for us to change the hearts and the destiny of the lost. Together we can give new life to those who live a life without prayer, making intercessors out of every believer to meet the needs of this generation.

CHAPTER 3 THREE

INTERCESSION WILL HOLD BACK THE PLAGUE

One reason prayer is such a necessity is that it can prevent natural disasters from occurring. One thing God told our prayer group over the years is that one of the greatest spirits we would combat in the last days would be the spirit of arson. Did you know that more people are intentionally setting fires these days than at any other time in the history of the world?

God can quench the violence of fires. Hebrews 11:34 says that the saints learned to quench the violence of fires by faith. However, God wants His people not only to quench natural fires, but also to quench the fires of hell through prayer.

Do you know where the fires of hell are actually lighted? They ignite in the hearts of men and women through vices such as drugs, alcohol, adultery, lust, and other horrible deceptions. Unfortunately, people are succumbing to the sins from the fires of hell as never before. But God has given His people a double portion of power to resist the wiles of the devil. We must learn to pull people "out of the fire; hating even the garment spotted by the flesh" (Jude 1:23).

Storms and tempests can be quieted through prayer. God told our prayer group that we had better learn how to deal with the elements of nature that would threaten us. We need not fear the hostile elements of nature. Satan may try to stir up the powers of the air, but they don't have to come near our dwelling places. (Ps. 91:7.)

I was in Tulsa on June 8, 1974, when a terrific storm was unleashed on the city, spawning multiple tornadoes that caused great damage. In the morning before that storm arrived, about 6:30 or 7 A.M., the Spirit of God, who knew what was ahead even before a cloud appeared in the sky, told me that something destructive was pending for the city. Well, I went into intercession all day long, and the Spirit of God rolled out of me with power. I cited instances in which men and women had stood before the Lord in prayer, saving nations of people. All day long I prayed like that, twelve hours in all.

The storm, tornadoes, and flooding hit the city, but Satan was not allowed to unleash the full brunt of the destruction he had planned. Later, I came across a newspaper article written by a meteorologist with the National Severe Storms Weather Center in Kansas City. The article reported that something had happened that seemed impossible. Apparently, there had been such a buildup of electrical intensity in the clouds above the city of Tulsa that officials could have spent seven months picking up the dead. However, a rapid change of some kind occurred that couldn't be explained, causing the storm to quickly die down in its intensity.

Let me tell you, this is the power of intercession! Through intercession, cities can be spared. We must be willing to give ourselves as living sacrifices unto God in prayer to change things from bad to good.

There may be earthquakes, tornadoes, and all types of calamities coming to this earth. As the body of Christ, you must be the patrol guard over your cities and nations! For example, when you hear that destructive forces are about to come against you or your city, you, as intercessors, need to stop them in the name of the Lord. Jesus did it, and so can you.

Satan would love to destroy the children of God, just as he tried to do to Job. But Job is named as one of the great intercessors of the Old Testament. (Ezek. 14:14,20.) The Scripture says that Job made intercession continually for his children. (Job 1:5.) Although Job felt alone, bewailing the fact that there were no other intercessors in his city, had it not been for his intercession, every one of those so-called "comforters" who had said the wrong things about God would have lost their lives. (Job 16:20,21.)

Have you ever encountered any of those "comforters" who say just the wrong thing at the wrong time? They can paint such a dark picture. You'd better watch out for Satan's magnifying glass; he has the wrong perspective on things, and he always magnifies the problem. Satan can blow problems way out of proportion.

But God's people don't have to be deceived by Satan, because they can hold back judgment through intercession. Many times in the Bible, one person held back God's judgment on an entire group of people. For example, Methuselah was a restrainer of the judgment of God. He died in April, one month before the great flood came of which Noah and his family were the only survivors![2] (Gen. 5:27.) Methuselah lived longer than anyone in the history of the world, and I believe that was because he held back the judgments of God.

The Bible also tells us that the church will hold back judgment in the last days. (2 Thess. 2:7.) In fact, the church has probably already begun holding back the judgments of God.

We are restrainers. We are the ones who hold the judgment back, and we can hold it back from interfering with many areas of our lives, even in the lives of our families.

Abraham held judgment back from his family. (Gen. 18:17- 33.) He kept interceding when the angels of the Lord came down to destroy Sodom and Gomorrah. (Gen. 19:27.) Lot, who was living in Sodom with his family at that time, didn't realize the peril he was in. But Abraham interceded on his behalf. And because of the intercession of one man, God spared a family. God sent angels to deliver Lot and his family out of Sodom. And when Lot's family didn't move fast enough to get out of the city, angels took them by the hand and coaxed them along. (Gen. 19:15,16.)

That is why people today shouldn't be worried about the Rapture. If God wouldn't begin to judge Sodom and Gomorrah until Lot and his family had gotten out of there, then how much more will He spare His church from the judgment by taking her up in the Rapture before the Great Tribulation? It is not a matter of pre-, mid-, or post-tribulation theory. God will not let His righteous family be harmed. Furthermore, Jesus would never get married without his bride. Therefore, the church will be spared the judgment of God.

WE MUST INTERCEDE FOR THE NATIONS

God is concerned about the plight of nations. He has a controversy to settle with the nations of the world, and that is to see sinners saved, delivered, and set free. The time for that settlement has come to pass. Hallelujah!

The coming of the Lord is upon us, and we will see God move more and more throughout the church to minister to the nations. He will begin to move this way in the nations as never before.

The problem is that many nations have become supremely devoted to the gratification of the flesh. When nations live only to enjoy whatever pleasure in which they can indulge themselves, then there is a plague of sin in the world.

When you see places that exist only to satisfy the lusts of the flesh, then you see a corresponding decline in morals. And when you see nations that are in moral decline, you will eventually see God's judgment follow.

I read an article that described a group of explorers who discovered many things in all four corners of the world. They discovered new continents, villages, people groups, and wealth untold, but they never discovered a sinless population.

You see, unredeemed human nature always follows after sin. That happens because of the original sin. Therefore, without Christ, any group of people— primitive or civilized—will turn to sin. That is why Jesus came.

FREEDOM IN CHRIST IS NOT A LICENSE TO SIN

When God brought the children of Israel out of Egypt, He wanted to teach them one lesson above all others. He wanted them to know that freedom did not give them license to sin. Rather, God gave them freedom to serve Him and one another in love.

We must decide to do what is right according to God's law of love. (Rom. 13:10.) We have a standard that is forever established in heaven. And by living according to this standard of life, which is Christ in us, we can be an obedient people with the freedom to please God and others.

Any time rebellion breaks out among God's people, you will find that it is brought about by selfishness. Rebellion brings discord, quarrels, division, strife, and every conceivable evil thing that displeases God.

Many Christians tell me today that they have come out of certain bondages to which they once had been addicted. However, sometimes after a few years, I find they have gone back into the very bonds God had once brought them out of. They did this because they mistakenly used their freedom as license to sin

Paul said, "What then? shall we sin, because we are not under the law, but under grace? God forbid" (Rom. 6:15). Sadly, however, because of grace, many have gone back to their drinking habits, their fornication, their adulteries, and their uncleanness.

A young man once told me a story about how he fell from grace. He said that after many years of being zealous for the things of God, he fell into sin. Now, even though this young man had graduated from a Bible college, he was battling uncleanness and an obscene tongue. All kinds of sin had found their way into his life.

I want to tell you something. I went to battle with those evil forces over this young man and fought the devil with him. And when we finished, that young man said, "I am free."

But I told him, "Not so fast. Yes, you are free now, but you must maintain this freedom God has given you. You must not in any way go back to those sins in your thought life. You must not let uncleanness enter your heart by way of your eye-gate. You must not in any way allow these forces to gain entrance into you."

God wants His people to be pure. The book of Numbers records Korah's rebellion, in which God opened the earth and 250 of the rebellion's ringleaders and their families were swallowed. (Num. 16:35.) The next day, the Israelites voiced their reaction to this act: "But on the morrow all the congregation of the children of Israel murmured against Moses and against Aaron, saying, Ye have killed the people of the Lord" (Num. 16:41). They mistakenly blamed the judgment of God on Moses and Aaron.

Do you know what will happen in these last days? God will again cleanse His church with the last rites of purification. These last days will be as those in the church's beginning, when Peter detected the lie of Ananias. The Spirit of the Lord revealed something that was wrong—something in disharmony with the will and nature of godly conduct. Peter discerned that Ananias was lying; and God judged it. Peter didn't discern this in the natural, but in the spirit. (Acts 5:1-11.) The consequences were severe: Ananias died.

You may say, "Oh, my, how terrible."

No, it isn't. It is better to get one rotten apple out of the basket than to allow it to rot all the others. Ananias's death was God's way of cleansing the church. Sin is a contaminating influence, and it must be eradicated.

You see, sin in the church is like mutiny on a ship at sea. When mutiny occurs onboard and everybody begins to rise up in rebellion against the captain, all the passengers and the very ship itself are endangered.

You may say, "I thought God was a God of mercy."

He is. Many of God's judgments and chastenings are acts of mercy. He sends judgment lest people go too far in sin and cross a line past which there is no return.

MOSES AND AARON'S INTERCESSION HELD BACK JUDGMENT

God heard the Israelites' murmuring; therefore, He called Moses and Aaron and told them He would wipe out all of the people.

And it came to pass, when the congregation was gathered against Moses and against Aaron, that they looked toward the tabernacle of the congregation: and, behold, the cloud covered it, and the glory of the Lord appeared. And Moses and Aaron came before the tabernacle of the congregation. And the Lord spake unto Moses, saying, Get you up from among this congregation, that I may consume them as in a moment. And they fell upon their faces.

And Moses said unto Aaron, Take a censer, and put fire therein from off the altar, and put on incense, and go quickly unto the congregation, and make an atonement for them: for there is wrath gone out from the Lord; the plague is begun. And Aaron took as Moses commanded, and ran into the midst of the congregation; and, behold the plague was begun among the people: and he put on incense, and made an atonement for the people. And he stood between the dead and the living; and the plague was stayed. Now they that died in the plague were fourteen thousand and seven hundred, beside them that died about the matter of Korah. And Aaron returned unto Moses unto the door of the tabernacle of the congregation: and the plague was stayed.

Numbers 16:42-50

I want you to know that God is still alive and well! He is able to, and He will, defend His Word regardless of what it takes.

God appeared in His glory to judge the rebellious Israelites. A great plague arose among them because of their transgression.

You have probably heard of the Asiatic plague, or the flu. Likewise, you have heard of the Bubonic plague, which destroyed multitudes of people. But the greatest plague of all erupted in heaven, where, in the very presence of God Himself, the plague of sin originated when Lucifer dared to rear his head in rebellion against God. (Isa. 14:13.)

We know that Goo immediately judged Lucifer and put down the rebellion in heaven. (v. 15.) Nevertheless, evil was unleashed. But God initiated a plan in which an intercessor came to earth as a sacrifice to stop the plague of sin. The plan of redemption had already been prepared before the foundation of the world.

Another plague, however, broke out in the Garden of Eden. Man was created with a free will, and he chose to disobey God, thereby unleashing the plague of disobedience. Once again, in His mercy, God came to the rescue, providing for mankind a way of escape from His judgment.

Once sin breaks out, either among a people, a church, or a nation, there is only one thing that can stop it: the blood of Jesus.

When sin breaks out, we must come to the altar of sacrifice, take a coal from that altar, and enter the presence of God, waving the censor of incense in His presence. This speaks to God of the only thing that satisfies His justice, and that is the blood of His Son, Jesus Christ. In our intercession, we plead the sacrifice of Jesus Christ, and the plague is stopped.

Temptation comes to everyone. The Old Testament recounts the story in which Satan provoked David and tempted him to count his army. Satan knew David's weak spot. He appealed to David's sense of pride. Satan said to David, *Wouldn't it be nice to say you have a million-man army?* Satan tempted David to take a census in Israel (1 Chron. 21:1), and at that time, only those men who were fit for battle were counted.

Now, David's general, Joab, cautioned David against taking the census (v. 3), but in the end Joab followed David's instructions. Joab had only begun the task when God said, "All right, if David is putting his confidence in numbers, then I will diminish them for him." (v. 7.)

You see, we should place our confidence in almighty God, not in numbers. However, sometimes we fail to do this. For example, sometimes we want to exaggerate and say, "I had 10,000 converts!" But we should not place such importance in numbers—neither should we trust in money or anything else, except God.

God was displeased with David, so He sent an angel with a sword to pass judgment. He slew 70,000 people. When David thought he would lose all his men, he suddenly became an intercessor! First Chronicles 21:16 says, "And David lifted up his eyes, and saw the angel of the Lord stand between the earth and the heaven, having a drawn sword in his hand stretched out over Jerusalem. Then David and the elders of Israel, who were clothed in sackcloth, fell upon their faces."

David had missed the mark. That is called sin. But instead of receiving full judgment, David received God's mercy. David, acting as an intercessor for his people, moved God to reduce the severity of judgment. Furthermore, David repented for his sins. David and the elders of Israel clothed themselves in sackcloth to signify their grief because of their sin. David always repented for his sin, and that is why God said David was a man after His own heart. (1 Sam. 13:14.)

And David said unto God, Is it not I that commanded the people to be numbered? even I it is that have sinned and done evil indeed; but

as for these sheep, what have they done? let thine hand, I pray thee, O Lord my God, be on me, and on my father's house; but not on thy people, that they should be plagued.

1 Chronicles 21:17

In essence, David was saying, "I'll give myself as a sacrifice until I see You move again on behalf of Your people." This type of prayer is the mark of a true intercessor. A true intercessor says, "I'll stand in their place." That is what Jesus did. That is what the ministry of Jesus was all about.

LET THE HOLY SPIRIT TAKE OVER

People have come to me asking all kinds of things. For example, people ask, "For what should I intercede? How do I intercede? Should I groan when I intercede?" Well, I have to say, forget terminology. Don't stop to worry about such techniques when the plague is coming on. Don't worry about whether you "moan" or "groan"— *just let the Holy Spirit flow!* The Holy Spirit knows what to pray for, and He'll direct your prayer to the place where it is needed the most.

People get so distracted by the technicalities that they don't know one prayer from another. When the plague strikes, there is no time to quarrel about technique. Just let the Holy Spirit take over. He knows how to handle the situation.

Look at Moses and Aaron's reaction to God's pronouncement of judgment on the Israelites. God was going to wipe them out, but Moses did not cross his arms and shake his head and say, "They probably deserve it!" No, that is *not* the way the intercessor looks at things. Moses and Aaron instead fell on their faces before the Lord, crying for mercy for the people. *The basic remedy for transgression is repentance and intercession.*

In Isaiah 53:12 we are told that Jesus "made intercession for the transgressors." Well, Jesus is still doing this today. Jesus and the Holy Spirit are interceding for every member of the church right now.

One area in which the church needs to direct its prayers today is the plague of sexual perversion. There is a plague of pornography and homosexuality that is trying to break up homes and destroy the youth of today. This plague is spreading, and if we don't intercede to stop it, our nation will become like Sodom and Gomorrah.

If you'll recall, Lot, who lived in Sodom, had no prayer life. The plague of perversion came right up to his door. If it hadn't been for Abraham, who maintained his intercessory prayer life before the presence of God, the perversion could have encroached into Lot's home and tainted him. Without prayer, he was no match for it. (Gen. 18:16-33; 19:1-24.)

Unfortunately, America suffers from its own plague. America is now being weighed in the balances and is coming up lacking. Nevertheless, God is saying to the intercessor, *The plague will come if you don't take a coal from the altar of sacrifice and begin praying for your people.*

You see, intercession simply means to stand in the gap—the breach caused by sin. An intercessor also repairs the breach between heaven and earth so that they can flow together once again in perfect unity.

When the plague comes, don't stand back and say, "There is nothing we can do." That is not true! There *is* something we can do. We can go forth in the name of Jesus, having our censors lit and filled with the coals of the passionate intercession, adopting the heart of Jesus Christ until this plague is stopped in our land!

We can accomplish this because One greater than Aaron has come among us: Jesus Christ, the Righteous One. He stood before the Father and said, "Father, if the plague of sin is not stopped, then it will destroy the human race. Let Your judgment fall on Me instead of them." Therefore, because Jesus willingly sacrificed Himself on our behalf as an act of intercession, the Father was pleased and the plague of sin was stopped. People can now be restored to the former high position of God's sons and daughters through their acts of repentance and intercession.

My brother was a musician who played with many of the big-name bands in the world. He was handsome, talented, and blessed with a brilliant mind. He could make the saxophone and clarinet sing when he played.

I loved my brother, but when I came to know Jesus, I realized my brother was an "infidel" according to the Bible. I urged him to believe in Jesus and read the Bible, but he always said, "That Book is God's wielding a stick at superstitious people."

Even though my brother was a skeptic, I interceded for him anyhow. One day while praying for my brother, I heard myself say, "Lord, I'll go to hell in his place if You will just save him." I was shocked when I heard this, even though it came from my own mouth. After a while, though, I realized that was the Holy Spirit speaking from the depth of love that Jesus had for the lost.

Well, I stepped in with a commitment to keep praying and standing in my brother's place before God. And before long, God broke the power of Satan over his life. I was able to see him come to the Lord and become filled with the Holy Spirit.

Thank God that as long as an intercessor is standing in the gap for unbelievers, Satan can't get to them. An intercessor holds Satan back and allows God's light to reach them.

Believe for your loved ones to come into the fullness of Christ! Mothers, dads, young people, stand in the gap until you see the lost come to repentance. You can do it! When you see a plague of any kind breaking out among your loved ones, there is only one thing that can stop it: Being willing to stand in the gap until repentance occurs.

Mankind was born to be free, but sin has made him choose to go back into slavery and bondage many, many times. This is the reason I want to show you the necessity of maintaining this beautiful prayer life in the church. Any plague can be stopped when the church becomes the great intercessory power she was meant to be.

CHAPTER FOUR

COMBATING THE
INTERCESSION
OF HELL

Did you know that hell makes intercession, just as the saints of God do? Specifically, the powers of darkness strive against believers on this earth. The good news is that Satan is defeated, and believers have authority over the devil. However, believers must still learn to enforce Satan's defeat. They must combat the powers of darkness with the truth that they do not wrestle against flesh and blood, but against principalities, powers, and the rulers of the darkness of this world. (Eph. 6:12.)

Luke 23:4-10 indicates that the powers of hell intercede against us. I had never understood this principle until the Holy Spirit quickened it to me one day, saying, *I want you to see hell's intercession.*

Oh, Lord! I thought. *I don't know if I want to see this.*

But He said, *Yes, go ahead and read it.*

What God showed me was that in the final week of Jesus' life on earth, Satan was making his last great stand against Jesus. He, of course, did not want Jesus to return to the throne in heaven, for Satan knew that if Jesus was at the Father's right hand, He would return there as a conqueror. To avert Jesus' conquest, the power of hell made its last attempt to kill Him as a man.

The devil knew that if Jesus arrived at the right hand of the Father, He would pour out the Holy Spirit upon the body of Christ. Then the powerful ministry of the church would be released upon the earth, overturning Satan's dominion and multiplying the works of Jesus' ministry.

Luke 23:1-5 gives the record of hell's intercession to kill Jesus:

> **And the whole multitude of them arose, and led him unto Pilate. And they began to accuse him, saying, We found this fellow perverting the**

nation, and forbidding to give tribute to Caesar, saying that he himself is Christ a King. And Pilate asked him, saying, Art thou the King of the Jews? And he answered him and said, Thou sayest it. Then said Pilate to the chief priests and to the people, I find no fault in this man.

Luke 23:1-4

Pilate didn't want to punish Jesus, but he also didn't want to go against public opinion. He must have sensed something about Jesus that told him Jesus was telling the truth, yet he was too weak in his convictions to stand against the pressure.

Public opinion is one of the strongest forces that can deter you from doing the will of God. Pilate had a little conviction to do the right thing when he first addressed the crowd that was assembled against Jesus. But without a strong conviction, he was unable to stand against the crowd. Thus, through the crowd, the powers of hell were able to make their reply against Jesus:

And they were the more fierce, saying, He stirreth up the people, teaching throughout all Jewry, beginning from Galilee to this place. When Pilate heard of Galilee, he asked whether the man were a Galilean. And as soon as he knew that he belonged unto Herod's jurisdiction,

he sent him to Herod, who himself also was at
Jerusalem at that time.

Luke 23:5-7

Thus, Herod took up issue against Jesus. Herod was the ruler of Galilee at the time of Jesus' crucifixion.

And the chief priests and scribes stood and
vehemently accused him. And Herod with his
men of war set him at nought, and mocked him,
and arrayed him in a gorgeous robe, and sent
him again to Pilate. And the same day Pilate and
Herod were made friends together: for before
they were at enmity between themselves.

Luke 23:10-12

It is amazing how some people get together on bad issues. Notice that it is always those who are the most religious—not the genuine Christians—who are the ones vehemently accusing Jesus.

And Pilate, when he had called together the
chief priests and the rulers and the people, said
unto them, Ye have brought this man unto me,
as one that perverteth the people: and, behold, I,
having examined him before you, have found no
fault in this man touching those things whereof
ye accuse him: no, nor yet Herod: for I sent you
to him; and, lo, nothing worthy of death is done

unto him. I will therefore chastise him, and release him. (For of necessity he must release one unto them at the feast.)

And they cried out all at once, saying, Away with this man, and release unto us Barabbas.

Luke 23:13-18

Here we see the powers of hell rising up among the people and making intercession on behalf of Satan against Jesus. The religious people of the day were saying, "Kill Him! We don't want Him to live. Crucify Him!"

Pilate tried three times to get the people to listen to reason, with no success. He realized there was no fault to be found in this Man, Jesus. Pilate knew the Jews had no cause for their accusations but, again, he didn't have a strong enough conviction to stand against them.

The will of Satan will always oppose Christ. And this will become more and more apparent as time comes to a close. Hell's intercessors will rise up when Christians stand against practices that are contrary to God's principles of life. Those wicked forces that rose up in the people against Jesus crying, "Get rid of that Man!" are still around today. Some of those same voices are now saying, "Get rid of God from public life!"

Isn't it strange that when Satan's crowd speaks out boldly against the things of God, they are generally tolerated, but when believers get somewhat vociferous, people usually tell them to shut up? The forces of hell are loud and brazen; therefore, the church must be bold to stand against them! The church of the living God must not let Satan have the final word!

PRAY IN THE SPIRIT TO BREAK THE FORCES OF EVIL

Through intercession, you can put pressure on satanic forces and break their power. The Bible says we don't wrestle against flesh and blood, but against principalities, powers, and the rulers of the darkness of this world. (Eph. 6:12.) Well, if they are interceding against us, crying out for us to be put down, how much more should we believers be interceding against them in the Holy Spirit?

The powers of hell are very efficient. Demons are very skillful and clever in their art. Therefore, we as believers must be that much more skillful and able to counteract their evil by the power of the Holy Spirit and the name of Jesus.

Paul wrote, "We know not what we should pray for as we ought: but the Spirit itself maketh intercession for us" (Rom. 8:26). Well, how does He do it? Of course, the Holy Spirit prays in accordance with the will of God. *There is only one way we can really know how to pray in league with God against the forces of evil, and that is when we are in the Spirit.*

Some people think the only powerful prayer is a loud one. In other words, people try to gauge a prayer's power by its volume. But, in reality, when people pray in the flesh, their prayers end up like firecrackers: They make a lot of noise, but they go out quickly. That type of prayer is *not* intercession.

In our church, we used to have an altar where people went at the end of a service to pray. Most of the time, when people went to that altar to pray, their heads were down but one eye was usually open, looking around to see if anyone was watching them.

For example, a certain man in the church would come down to the altar and even get down on one knee because he loved the spotlight so much. He would explode in prayer for about five minutes, and then he was done. Any other time when prayer was needed, no one could find him. The only time he wanted to pray was in front of others.

You see, there is very little about a prayer bellowed out randomly that truly emanates from the mind and heart of God. If that were so, more churches would be alive because of this kind of prayer. However, true intercession involves praying to combat the forces of evil, not to parade around spouting off prayers halfheartedly to impress people. As we have already seen, "The effectual fervent prayer of a righteous man availeth much" (James 3:16).

That is good to know because we need that kind of power. We need to be dangerous to the powers of hell, just as Paul was. His ministry was so powerful against the forces of hell that the mob at Asia said, "Mark that man."

And when the seven days were almost ended, the Jews which were of Asia, when they saw him in the temple, stirred up all the people, and laid hands on him, crying out, Men of Israel, help: This is the man, that teacheth all men every where against the people, and the law, and this place: and further brought Greeks also into the temple, and hath polluted this holy place. (For they had seen before with him in the city Trophimus an Ephesian, whom they supposed that Paul had brought into the temple.)

And all the city was moved, and the people ran together: and they took Paul, and drew him out of the temple: and forthwith the doors were shut. And... they went about to kill him.

Acts 21:27-31

Hell is violent. But it can never agree with itself. It can never sustain a unified message:

> **Then the commander came near and took him [Paul]... and he asked who he was and what he had done. And some among the multitude cried one thing and some another. So when he could not ascertain the truth because of the tumult, he commanded him to be taken into the barracks.**
>
> **Acts 21:33,34** NKJV

The reason many of us today aren't as outspoken as Paul was is that we are either too complacent or too afraid to disturb the gates of hell as Paul did. We're too much at ease in Zion today. Hell is violent against the church, and the church needs to be violent in return.

Matthew 11:12 says, "And from the days of John the Baptist until now the kingdom of heaven suffereth violence, and the violent take it by force." That is how we must combat hell. We must be so empowered by praying God's will in these end times that we drive back the powers of hell and set people free. We must never become apathetic as we combat hell's intercession.

Hell is out to destroy God's people by foul means or fair ones. For example, when you see a church that has a real touch of God upon her, beware! Don't think that just because a church has the beautiful touch of God, people will be able to sit back and do nothing to maintain it. Even Paul said as much when he was speaking to the believers at Miletus. He said, "For I know this, that after my departing shall grievous wolves enter in among you, not sparing the flock" (Acts 20:29). But, praise God, we have the victory over the enemy and can triumph in any situation. (2 Cor. 2:14.)

WE MUST GET TO KNOW THE FATHER THROUGH PRAYER

Did you know that just because you know the *letter* of the Word doesn't mean you know the Word *Himself?* The Jews, for example, could quote the first five books of the Bible verbatim. Yet, on the day of Pentecost, it was the Gentiles whom the Holy Spirit swept into the life of Christ!

This tells us that being acquainted with the letter of the law alone kills. (2 Cor. 3:6.) But knowing the Holy Spirit brings spiritual life. Furthermore, knowing the Father personally makes the letter of the Word come alive. And with this life, real spiritual work can be accomplished!

Jesus gives His resurrection life as the Holy Spirit administers the Word. That is good news, because the Bible should be more than just a mere book to Christians. It is the Word that brings life, and Jesus is the Word made flesh. With His divine life within us by the power of the Holy Spirit, we can accomplish anything at all for eternity and the glory of Jesus Christ!

Unfortunately, as Christians we often reach a certain spiritual level and begin to feel that we are beyond the need to humble ourselves at the feet of Jesus and His cross. Not only that, but sometimes we can even get so filled with pride that we believe we are actually on a higher spiritual level than everyone else is. When this happens, we are less likely to humble ourselves in prayer before Almighty God.

Remember that as long as Jesus was a Man on earth, He was totally dependent on His Father in heaven. Moreover, the authority and the works Jesus displayed came from the power of the Holy Spirit as it flowed through Him because He lived in constant contact with the Father. Hebrews 5:7 says, "Who in the days of his flesh, when he had offered up prayers and supplications with strong crying and tears unto him that was able to save him from death, and was heard in that he feared."

You can't get any higher than that, can you? Jesus our King is God's own Son and was destined to become the King of kings. Yet He had the greatest prayer life of any man who ever walked the face of the earth. He lived His life in the flesh dependent upon the Father, just as you and I should.

Jesus will never ask us to do anything He Himself did not do first. Likewise, we must never ask anyone to put on a yoke that we're not willing to bear ourselves. For example, whenever I hear ministers give exhortations on prayer, I first watch to see if they carry out what they say in their own lives. Sometimes I find they are the first ones off their knees and out the door. Ironically, however, these are also the ones telling other people how much they need to pray.

Let me tell you a story that illustrates this point. In Old Testament days, the kings led their people into battle. King David was always there to lead Israel in war. But when he stayed home from battle just once, David got into trouble. (2 Sam. 11:1-4.)

You see, in the Old Testament, the anointing only came upon those who fulfilled the office to which they were called. Therefore, when David didn't go into battle, he lost his anointing. He operated in the flesh and became subject to sin.

Well, because we are in Christ, we are not only kings upon the earth, but we are priests and prophets too. Therefore, as kings, priests, and prophets, we are being led into battle with the anointing of the Holy Spirit to win!

INTERCESSION REMOVES THE VEIL OF SPIRITUAL BLINDNESS

When you're fighting the forces of hell in prayer, you must resolve to never give up! Never allow defeat even to enter your mind. Know that no matter how long it takes, if God has said it and promised it, then it *will* come to pass! Spiritual sight will be restored to the blind, and spiritual hearing will be restored to the deaf.

You may sometimes feel as though you are opposing hell's intercession by yourself, but Jesus is your High Priest and Chief Intercessor. Hell may cry out for the destruction of your soul, but Jesus is on your side. Satan wants to keep you in blindness; but he can't because Jesus has already given you spiritual sight and set you free.

At one time, Satan was vested with the authority and powers of judgment. He was able to render decisions.

But Satan turned from God and set up a world system in which he blinds men's spiritual eyes to their need for God. Satan, the former anointed cherub who ministered at the throne of God, now attempts to cast his covering over the nations on earth and over the hearts of men. But the Bible speaks of the breaking of that covering, that veil: "And he will destroy in this mountain the face of the covering cast over all people, and the vail that is spread over all nations" (Isa. 25:7). Satan's covering will be broken by the power of the blood of Jesus Christ through intercession.

That is why Satan did not want to see Jesus fulfill the plan of redemption. That is why Satan manipulated the crowds to condemn Jesus to death. Under Satan's influence, the crowds refused to give up, contending for judgment until Jesus was put to death. (Luke 23.)

These same satanic influences exist among people today. But that is where the church intervenes with intercession. The church can come against these evil influences in the name of Jesus.

Through prayer, the church can reconcile two parties who are separated by differences-namely, the world and God. To do this, the intercessors must know both parties. Christian intercessors must understand both how God thinks and how the unsaved person thinks in order to bring the two together. Intercessors will learn to know things about God by spending time in His presence, and they can then take this knowledge to mankind.

Moses was a true intercessor. He learned how to approach both God and man. Moses would stand before God when God was about to destroy an entire race of people, actually putting himself in the middle. God said, "Get out of the way, Moses, and let Me get to them!" (Ex. 32:7-10.)

But God can't pour out His judgment when an intercessor is standing in the way. The intercessor is the middleman. He stands between the living God and those who are spiritually dead and in need of the life Jesus gives. An intercessor brings two together who have been separated by differences.

God and man were once separated. Sin raised a barrier between them. God couldn't reach man, and man couldn't reach God. So God said, *I have to deal with this barrier, this roadblock. I have to get it out of the way so I can continue the divine plan and purpose I had in mind when I created mankind.* And God sent Jesus to go between the two parties.

An intercessor knows both God and man and brings the two together. As an intercessor, Moses would fall on his face before almighty God and reverse His judgment. When God had decreed destruction for His people, it was Moses who asked God not to do it. And God finally said, "Okay, Moses, get up. I won't do this."

If you want to be an intercessor, you have to know your God as Moses did. You have to know how to be bold in His presence.

PUT THE ENEMY UNDER YOUR FEET

Long ago God told us as intercessors that the birth pangs would begin "in the hidden parts." That represents the closet of our intercession. Let me tell you what I mean by that. Often the Holy Spirit would show our prayer group things from a long-range perspective. Like watchmen on a wall, we would see events to come.

You see, hell doesn't want intercessors to continue their prayers. But even though Satan may try to thwart God's intercessors, just as he sought to destroy Jesus, he can't. Hell's forces may be vehement, loud, and persistent, but God's intercessors already have the victory in Christ.

When we wrestle against an opponent, one who wants to keep us down, we don't need to lose heart. We wrestle in the Spirit, just as David wrestled against Goliath. David conquered Goliath by faith and determination, knowing that his opponent was already a defeated foe. Remember that when David slew Goliath, he approached the giant and put his foot on Goliath's neck. That is what the Bible calls putting the enemy under your feet! (Rom. 16:20.)

Through the power of the Holy Spirit, intercessors hold on to God with one hand and on to man with the other. In this way, they overcome the powers, principalities, and rulers of the darkness of this world! By entering into partnership with God like this, interceding believers can gain the ascendancy in times of trouble!

As saints, we don't have to take what hell dishes out! The power and grace of God are not limited only to our personal salvation from sin, but it can operate in every aspect of our lives. If it weren't for the power and grace of God, we wouldn't be able to function in this fallen world. Satan wouldn't let us. But because Jesus came and conquered the devil, we are capable of doing all that God asks of us! And we will be able to do even more as His coming nears.

If only we could fully realize the vastness of God's grace toward us. It is God's desire for us to come to the full stature of our development in Christ, to qualify us for a kingly position in His kingdom!

A WINNING COMBINATION: THE WORD AND PRAYER

The birth pangs of a new age are upon us. We are in the closing days of this current dispensation. But always in the dying of one day, another day breaks forth. The light of a new day is beginning to dawn. So don't give up! Break through the veil of darkness by prayer and faith with the power of the Word and the Holy Spirit.

There must be a balance between the two. We cannot have the Word without prayer, and we cannot pray effectively without the Word. The two work together; they are joined eternally. "What therefore God hath joined together, let not man put asunder" (Matt. 19:6).

PRIVATE PRAYER IS THE KEY TO PUBLIC MINISTRY

Jesus began His ministry with prayer, and He closed it with prayer. Furthermore, He prayed all the time in between. However, He never did much praying in public. Here is a secret that we can learn from His example. Jesus prayed in His quiet times *before* He went out publicly. That is one of the reasons He had such phenomenal power.

If we want to enjoy successes like Jesus did, we must pray as He prayed. We need to do our homework behind the scenes—unless otherwise instructed by the Holy Spirit. It is often too easy for prayer in public to become merely something to fill time in a service and to impress the people. That is not the way Jesus prayed at all.

I knew a minister who had such a great anointing that when the Spirit of God would come upon him and he would begin to intercede, no one had to give an altar call at all. People just flocked to the altar themselves. They recognized that this man had been with Jesus, and they came to the altar when he prayed.

You see, it isn't necessary to tell people that you spend hours in prayer—they will already know if you do. People will know you have been in the presence of Jesus. When you go out in public, the Holy Spirit will confirm and verify the fact that you have been with Jesus. It will be apparent to everyone, just as was the fragrance upon the Old Testament priest who had spent time in the Holy of Holies. (Ex. 30:34-37.)

The priest who ministered at the altar of incense departed with the scent of the incense upon him. As the incense rose from the altar, it permeated every part of him: his hair, his clothing, his face, and his eyes. When he came out, everyone knew where he had been—in the Holy Place. (Ex. 30:6-8; Lev. 16:12,13.)

Remember, every one of you has a divine right to be a bearer of lift and light. God is the giver of light, and intercessors are a saving force in the earth. You can hold back judgment. You can release ministries and finances. You can save cities if God so wills. And you can even extend time just as King Hezekiah did when he prayed. (Isa. 38:5.)

I count it the greatest privilege to be an intercessor for God. I'm not ordained by man to do what I'm doing, because I don't need a person's approval. I remain a free woman to pray as I will. I'm just a layperson like many of you. But, oh, what God can do with a layperson!

You don't have to be an ordained preacher to do mighty works for the Lord. All you have to do is be a lay witness for God. That is all He wants.

LET JESUS BE YOUR TEACHER

There is so much to know about the life of God, and we certainly don't know it all yet. I found out that many of the things I learned years ago were things I had memorized and could repeat by rote like a parrot. Often, I just imitated other people. But things changed over the years as I sat at Jesus' feet and learned of Him. That interaction with Him is the one thing that is dearest to my heart. It is called intercession.

Jesus is coming soon! It was said of David's soldiers from the tribe of Issachar that they had "an understanding of the times" (1 Chron. 12:32). Furthermore, Jesus said the day of the Lord should not "come upon you unawares" (Luke 21:34).

You are not children of darkness. You are children of the light. (1 Thess. 5:5.) Because of this, "that day" should not take you unawares. Through careful study and sensitivity to the Holy Spirit, you will find out that God did not leave us in the dark concerning Christ's return. And as saints, we need to offset hell's darkness with our light.

I'm a mother, grandmother, and housewife, but I'm also a counselor, prayer worker, and most important of all, an intercessor.

But do you know what God showed me about fulfilling all of these roles? Lately God has shown me what was required in the Old Testament era. He reminded me of a practice He told the Israelites to follow when they worked their land. God required that the land be allowed to rest for certain periods of time. And each time the Israelites failed to do this, they were taken into captivity.

This is a principle God requires not only for land, but for us as well. The fact is that we will take a rest one way or another. In other words, if we don't voluntarily take some time out to rest, we may come to a place where our bodies shut down and we are forced to rest. This can happen whether we like it or not.

God told me that the reason this principle applies to us as well as to land is that we are made from natural elements-the dust of the ground. God created us that way. Therefore, it would be wise for us to learn how to rest and take a Sabbath day off.

THE PROMISES OF GOD COME TO FRUITION THROUGH INTERCESSION

The promises of God will be fulfilled if people will pray. As we have already seen, Daniel read the biblical prophecies and saw that the time for his people to be released from captivity was near. He desired to see his people return to their own land, so he committed to prayer and fasting. He interceded for his people, that God would bring His promise of freedom to pass. And as Daniel prayed, he had a visitation from God in which he was given great prophecies. (Dan. 9:2-27.)

God's Word teaches us that we will see the time of the coming of the Lord approaching. And why shouldn't we? Spiritually alert saints helped to pray the modern state of Israel into existence. Likewise, the saints today can help bring into existence an understanding of end-time events.

Prayer will help bring Jesus back to set up His kingdom on earth. And we need Jesus to cone back, because the world will never know real peace until He comes again. Just talking about His return is not enough. What we really need to do is lay hold of the horns of the altar in prayer, believing God to bring forth the fulfillment of His promises.

Yes, we have the Word, and, yes, we have the promises. But it is up to us as the body of Christ to bring God's prophecies into manifestation through our prayers. It may take work. It may take intercession like the travail a woman undergoes during the birth of a child, but we must not give up until it is fulfilled. (Mic. 4:10.)

Praying like this does have a cost. I won't lie to you; the Bible speaks about offering your body up to God's service as a living sacrifice, holy and acceptable unto God. (Rom. 12:1.) If you aren't willing to make such a sacrifice, you are an unprofitable servant. (Luke 17:10.) As a member of the church of the living God, you cannot just sit back and watch the war from the sidelines. The mark of a real Christian is the mark of an intercessor!

We Christians in America live in the greatest land on earth. If only the church knew how to intercede on behalf of our nation! We have such a great opportunity to bless others, but we also have an awesome responsibility. If only we Christians in America would give ourselves to intercession for this country, God could turn the tide of our nation. Judgment could be held back by intercession.

GOD WILL PROTECT AND GUIDE HIS INTERCESSORS

Look at some of the great intercessors of the Bible. Abraham and Noah, for example, both held back judgment in their day, and they couldn't even pray in the Holy Spirit! How much more, then, can we as New Testament believers hold back judgment that would otherwise come to our unbelieving sons, daughters, or relatives! Our standing in the gap and building up the hedge of protection makes the difference!

Jeremiah, the weeping prophet, was God's oracle to the house of Israel in the last days before the captivity of Babylon. He once said, "Oh that my head were waters, and mine eyes a fountain of tears, that I might weep day and night for the slain of the daughter of my people!" (Jer. 9:1). Jeremiah interceded for God's people.

Well, did you know that when the pagan Babylonians conquered Jerusalem, the captain of Nebuchadnezzor's host said, "Don't touch Jeremiah"? The prophet was released to go wherever he wanted. He was not a captive. The captain made provision for all of Jeremiah's material needs. (Jer. 40:4,5.) Jeremiah was a great intercessor, and God protected him because he had drawn close to the golden altar of incense.

If you seek this kind of protection, seek also the very beating of God's heart. You will find them both in the secret place of the Most High. That is the call of the intercessor—to know Him.

In the Old Testament era, the high priest could not enter the presence of God without incense or the blood of an animal. As we know, incense is a type of the prayers of God's people, and blood is a symbol of holiness. These priests could not go into God's presence without blood or incense. Today we cannot go into God's presence without prayer and holiness, the covering and cleansing of Jesus' blood.

Intercession is such a privilege. The Holy Spirit confers such an honor upon you as you intercede for others: He gives you revelation knowledge. Jesus said the Holy Spirit would show you things to come and guide you into *all truth*. (John 16:13.) He guides you into this truth as you pray, spending time with the Father.

AN OBLIGATION TO BATTLE IN THE SPIRIT

I remember when God called me to emergency intercession during the Vietnam War. I thought to myself, *If men can go to war in the natural to preserve my freedom, then I'm willing to go to war in the Spirit for them.* If those soldiers would fight for me, willing to live or die on a foreign battlefield, I had an obligation to go to battle in the Spirit against the forces that wanted to destroy our men and our nation.

So that is what I did. I gave myself to intercession for the war in Vietnam, standing in the gap to see God come on the scene in His might and power.

God showed our prayer group some amazing things when we began to pray for Vietnam. For example, once when we were in intercession, I found myself standing before world rulers, commanding them to free the prisoners of war. Other times God would reveal to us the daily movements of those we loved in Vietnam.

One such person was a prisoner of war named Lieutenant Colonel Robinson Risner. He had grown up in my Sunday school class and was a good man, a man of God. I said to God, "Lord, if those men can fight over there and suffer for us, then I am willing to give myself to fighting for them over here in the Spirit. Together we can set them free!"

The Holy Spirit showed me some of the POW camps in Vietnam. I have seen them, and I have seen those prisoners by the power of the Holy Spirit. God told us that when some of them were just about ready to give up, we had to pray. God would say, *Tonight I will render a concert for them.* So that night our prayer group sang some of the most beautiful songs we knew. God told us He would relay them to the POWs by the Holy Spirit. He told us their spirits would be revived, and I wondered how this could be.

Well, some time later, I read the God had ministered to a pastor who was a prisoner in the communist camps. God told him to stay awake at night and sleep during the day, because the communists were active in the daytime. But at night, when all was quiet, God took him by the Holy Spirit to places in America where church services were being held. And God let him be a part of those services. In that way, he was spiritually fed and blessed.

PRAYER WILL BRING THE CHURCH TO HER FULL STRENGTH AND STATURE

Ephesians tells us that God equips the church with various ministry gifts:

And he gave some, apostles; and some, prophets; and some, evangelists; and some, pastors and teachers; for the perfecting of the saints, for the work of the ministry, for the edifying of the body of Christ: till we all come in the unity of the faith, and of the knowledge of the Son of God, unto a perfect man, unto the measure of the stature of the fulness of Christ.

Ephesians 4:11-13

Paul saw his own people fail to come into full maturity in Christ. He mentioned this very fact in Galatians, saying, "My little children, of whom I travail in birth again until Christ be formed in you" (Gal. 4:19).

In essence, Paul said that it is not enough just to be born again without growing into full maturity in Christ. God has a measure of growth that He desires for every individual and generation to attain. Reaching that level must be our aspiration.

I'm convinced that the coming of the Lord will soon be ushered in. The glorious church will reach full maturity for her bridegroom. He will not marry a baby; He will marry the bride who has grown into her full stature. She must be equal to the privilege of sitting at His right hand.

MINING THE GEMS OF THE SPIRIT

God finds intercessors who will toil until what God has planned has manifested. God gave our prayer group a wonderful example by comparing intercessory prayer with the mining of the earth. God revealed that intercessors are much like miners. They travel deep underground, where no one can see them. People on the surface cannot see what they're doing, and they are

often overlooked or forgotten. Yet these miners go
where few others will tread in order to seek out caverns
of treasure. These minerals are used to keep industries
running, homes heated, people clothed, jobs supplied,
and so forth. If this energy resource were not supplied,
all major activity on the surface of the earth would slow
to a halt.

Well, when we began our intercessory prayer group
in the early 1960s, God told us we would be like the
miners who go underground, unearthing precious
minerals for those who live on the surface of the earth.
Many times an intercessor's work is overlooked. Yet
intercessors are willing to go underground in the Spirit
to dig out precious gems to keep God's plan going, to
dig out the "coal of the Spirit" to fuel God's economy.
What a blessing!

CHAPTER FIVE

EFFECTUAL PRAYER

Jesus is our great example for everything that we do. And even though He is our High Priest, while He was here on the earth He operated as a man who was dependent upon the Holy Spirit. So we must ask ourselves how Jesus had the power to perform the signs and wonders that He did.

Jesus was born of the Spirit, but He still had to maintain continual contact with the Father through prayer. He was able to perform such miraculous signs and wonders because the Holy Spirit produced them through Him.

Hebrews 5:7 says, "Who in the days of his flesh, when he had offered up prayers and supplications with strong crying and tears unto him that was able to save him from death, and was heard in that he feared." This Scripture is not telling us that Jesus was afraid of God the Father. Rather, Jesus so respected and relied upon the Father to perform the works that He continually kept His communication with Him intact.

James describes our own need to remain in constant contact with the Father: "Confess your faults one to another, and pray one for another, that ye may be healed. The effectual fervent prayer of a righteous man availeth much" (James 5:16). What is the "effectual fervent prayer" James is talking about?

If all the prayers that believers have prayed throughout history had been "effectual fervent prayers," the entire world would be knocking down the doors of the church to get saved. But sadly, most of our prayers have been just for show. Rarely do we pray in private. And when we do come out in public to pray, we tend to speak forth our prayers with pomp and ceremony. But if our prayers are just lip service, we'd be better off not wasting our breath! So many people's lives depend on effectual, fervent prayers that we can't afford to pray ineffectually.

When Jesus taught the disciples about prayer, He told them that most of their prayers should not be made publicly. (Matt. 6:6.) In our society, there are many things that should not be displayed publicly, such as intimate displays of affection between people. Those don't belong in public, and neither does intimate communion with the Father. This kind of prayer belongs either among the safety of believers or in the privacy of the prayer closet, where spiritual battles are fought and won. Prayer in the secret place should come first, where few people notice; and then the victory will come in the open battlefield, where people are saved, filled with the Holy Spirit, healed, and delivered.

Too often we pray loudly in public, trying to twist God's arm to do what He has promised instead of spending quality, private time with Him first. This is the reason why many prayers are ineffectual.

THE REASON WE PRAISE GOD

One day God revealed to me a reason for praising Him that I had not known before. He told me, *The reason it is good for you to praise Me is not that it benefits Me, but because it benefits you, and it prevents Satan from getting glory.* Praising God prevents Satan from taking any of the glory! In the very beginning, it was Satan's desire to become God, taking God's place in heaven. And when Satan fell, he said, "I will ascend into heaven, I will exalt my throne above the stars of God: I will sit also upon the mount of the congregation, in the sides of the north: I will ascend above the heights of the clouds; I will be like the most High" (Isa. 14:13,14.)

God revealed to me that Satan constantly seeks praise for himself. He craves attention, and he covets praise. But when you give praise to God, you're saying to Satan, "God is my God, not you!" God assured me that He doesn't require praise because He is egotistical, and it is not true that He won't do anything for you unless you praise Him. That is not the way God is. But praising God lets Satan know who God is! When you give God praise, Satan flees because he knows it is God you are worshiping, not him.

So, it is this communion with God through praise and effectual, fervent prayer that really does "avail much." This kind of expression to and communion with God really does cause things to happen.

Look at the life of Elijah, for example. Elijah prayed and caused the heavens to be shut up so that there was no rain during the reign of King Ahab. (1 Kings 17:1.) But when the time of drought was over, Elijah prayed again. The Bible says, "And it came to pass in the mean while, that the heaven was black with clouds and wind, and there was a great rain" (1 Kings 18:45).

The drought that Elijah prophesied can be compared to the state of the world today. Just as the earth needs natural rain, the lost need spiritual rain. They are dying because they need a Holy Ghost rain! In fact, they need a spiritual flood!

This is the reason the Bible says, "Ask ye of the Lord rain in the time of the latter rain; so the Lord shall make bright clouds, and give them showers of rain, to every one grass in the field" (Zech. 10:1). God said, "Ask, and it shall be given you" (Matt. 7:7). God wants us to ask for spiritual rain to fall so that the harvest may be brought to maturity and so that the church may be brought to her full stature in Christ.

God's church was actually born after a great prayer meeting. She waited for ten days in God's presence until suddenly there came a sound from heaven like a rushing mighty wind that filled the place. (Acts 2:2.) After that, a great revival resulted when Peter arose on the Day of Pentecost and preached that marvelous sermon to the multitude at Jerusalem.

The book of Acts describes the results of their united prayer:

Then they that gladly received his word were baptized: and the same day there were added unto them about three thousand souls.

**And they continued steadfastly in the apostles'
doctrine and fellowship, and in breaking of
bread, and in prayers.**

Acts 2:41,4

Prayer has always played an important role in the
lives of those who serve God. Exodus 30:8 outlines
instructions for keeping the tabernacle, which serves as
a type of prayer for us today. The priests were to never
let the incense die out in the holy place; it was to be "a
perpetual incense before the Lord throughout your
generations." Prayer is to constantly rise into God's
presence as an acceptable work of mankind. He taught
us by the example of the golden altar of incense that in
the church of the living God, prayer is never to go out.

God gave us these instructions for a reason. He
knows the end from the beginning, and He wants His
church to continue in prayer until the end.

The book of Revelation speaks of the end of
church history and foretells how the church will
complete her journey. But the beginning of the book of
Revelation reveals certain messages to the churches,
and the news is not so good. Great changes have come
to the churches that were once strong in prayer. They
have grown cold. The great Ephesian church, for
example, which had reached a high pinnacle of

spiritual knowledge, has become so cold that Jesus says to her, "You have lost your first love." (Rev. 2:4.) In this passage, it is the church, not the individual sinner, whom Jesus calls to repentance.

If we have access to the power of prayers that avail much but we do not use it, then we are in sin. We sin against the people in our generation when we don't pray for them. If we don't pray for our church, their light can become dim, and they can lose their first love.

Did you know that China was once one of the most enlightened Christian nations in the world? She once sent many missionaries to spread the gospel around the world. Yet, because of her unwillingness to continue to walk in the light of the gospel, she has plunged into virtually total spiritual darkness.

Sadly, this has happened in other nations as well. Look at the modern nation of Iran, for example. People from this nation (called "Persians" in the Bible) were present on the Day of Pentecost. (Acts 2:5.) This revival touched them, and they could have taken it back to their country, watered it with prayer and the Word, and caused a mighty change in their land. Sadly, however, the gospel's light slowly set in that nation.

The light of the gospel moves much the same as sunlight moves across the earth. The gospel has moved across the whole world, and many nations have walked in it. However, if they refuse to continue in that light, it will move on.

You see, we all only have twenty-four hours each day in which to shine for God. God gives everyone an equal opportunity to maintain the light of the gospel. But just as the sun moves across each continent in the span of a day, the light of God's visitation will move on if it is not esteemed.

> **Yet a little while is the light with you. Walk while ye have the light, lest darkness come upon you: for he that walketh in darkness knoweth not whither he goeth. While ye have light, believe in the light, that ye may be the children of light.**
>
> **John 12:35,36**

The doors of opportunity are great for us today! Effectual, fervent prayer can change things, but so often people do not want to pay the price. The Bible says, "Greater love hath no man than this, that a man lay down his life for his friends" (John 15:13). So, how much do you want true communion with the Father? It is obvious God wanted a relationship with you so much that He was willing to send His only Son to lay down His life for you.

He is not necessarily asking us to lay down our lives in death, but we are asked to lay down some of our trivial, selfish behaviors that prevent us from praying for the lost. Even certain social obligations, which may seem important to us, are preventing us from taking time to pray for the lost.

I should know. I was a person who loved the world. I loved the excitement of social activities and being with people. I loved tennis; I loved football; I loved soccer; I loved dancing; I loved music; and I loved the theater. I just loved it all!

But when God came to me in His beautiful and glorious presence in 1961, saying, *Daughter, would you be willing to give yourself in intercession for your nation and for the people of God until there comes again a mighty move of God in the earth? Would you be willing to leave all of those worldly things behind?* I couldn't resist. I loved Him more than my social calendar. Now, don't think it is wrong to fellowship with others in the body of Christ. It isn't. But God asked me to leave all that behind for a reason.

I had actually served God almost thirty years at that point. I taught a young married people's Sunday school class, and I just loved to socialize with them!

But God said, *I don't want you to touch one part of the social life of this church until I tell you to. Would you be willing to do that?* Well, I was.

God didn't force me to cut back on my social activities. He isn't a dictator. He has a Father's heart. But He wanted to know if I would join Him in the Spirit's great activity of proclaiming the kingdom of heaven on earth.

It shocked me one day when God said to me, *I want you to give up all public ministry until I call you back into it.* I responded by saying, "God, by Your grace—and by Your grace alone—I'll do what you want me to do." Thus, I ended my public teaching ministry. I did nothing but intercession. There was a small group who came with me, and we bonded together. Our little nucleus of intercessors prayed together until 1981.

For six years during that time, I was in intercession day and night, throughout the height of the Cold War and the Vietnam War. During that time God told me, *Because of your command in prayer, you will help bring into the world things of heaven beyond your comprehension.* It was so exciting to me. Those years spent in prayer were so thrilling, so marvelous, and so wonderful. I wouldn't trade them for anything in the world.

Yes, it took discipline to remain in prayer that way. It took self-denial. There were times, especially at night, when I would have liked to have gone places with the members of my family. But when I did make the sacrifice to obey God and pray, God always shined a bright light upon my pathway, reminding me of the Scripture, "The effectual fervent prayer of a righteous man availeth much" (James 5:16).

How much do you love the people of this world? I love them so much that I would do anything by God's grace to see them set free. Some people can reel the Word off their tongues, but that alone doesn't get people saved. The Jews knew the Word. They could quote it verbatim, and yet, they sinned by not praying with a heart full of love for the Lord.

Israel could have been spared years of captivity had they prayed with sincere hearts, turning to the Lord in repentance. But despite all of God's promises and dealings with the Jews, they wouldn't turn from their iniquities. God even called the prophet Jeremiah to plead with them, giving them one last chance before allowing them to be taken into captivity. God said, "Call unto me, and I will answer thee, and shew thee great and mighty things, which thou knowest not" (Jer. 33:3).

But they would not repent and exercise one of the highest functions of their spiritual natures, prayer. They refused to pray to the Father.

Daniel said, "Therefore hath the Lord watched upon the evil, and brought it upon us: for the Lord our God is righteous in all his works which he doeth: for we obeyed not his voice" (Dan. 9:14). Daniel knew Israel's only way to avert the catastrophe that was about to come was for the people to pray and turn from iniquity. He also knew that if they would not take this way out, then God could not be blamed.

Be reminded that God's promises are not only to you, but also to your children and to your children's children, if you walk in obedience. (Gen. 28:4.) It is your business to be obedient to fulfill God's call when the light shines on your pathway.

You see, prayer can hold back all kinds of calamity. Prayer can hold back judgment both from nations and from individuals. By praying, husbands can prevent harm from coming to their wives and children. Wives can avert danger from entering their husbands' paths. Mothers and fathers can pray their children into peace and safety.

Satan would just love to destroy every one of us. But he can't, if we are in proper fellowship with the Father. The devil can't touch God's people when they are protected by prayer and obedience. Remember when Daniel was thrown into the den of lions? (Dan. 6:11-24.) That was the devil's attempt to kill Daniel. But it failed because Daniel was a man of prayer, and he was found innocent before the Lord and the king of Babylon.

> **My God hath sent his angel, and hath shut the lions' mouths, that they have not hurt me: forasmuch as before him innocency was found in me; and also before thee, O king, have I done no hurt.**
>
> **Daniel 6:22**

Prayer and obedience to God kept Daniel alive. Prayer is one of the greatest forms of preservation and protection that an individual can utilize. Therefore, we should take our responsibility seriously and pray regularly for our families and for whomever God directs us.

Praying to God should be as natural for you as breathing. You don't have to say to your lungs, "Breathe! I have got to have some air!" No, your lungs are designed by God to automatically breathe in the air that you need to live.

I have found that if you will train your spirit to pray—which is actually a natural thing for your spirit to do—then in quiet times the Holy Spirit of God will prompt you to pray as often as necessary. John 9:4 says, "The night cometh, when no man can work." That verse is spiritually referring to the Tribulation, but there is a natural application to that truth as well. The Holy Spirit can wake you in the night to pray if need be. He never slumbers nor sleeps and is aware of all that is going on. He is the watchman on your wall.

I have trained my spirit to be so sensitive to the Holy Spirit that He has awakened me in the night so I could pray. The Holy Spirit usually does this when He knows the enemy is ready to attack.

One night, for example, I saw this awful creature in the spirit that was just about ready to attack me. But the Holy Spirit, who was on duty while I was asleep, awakened me and alerted me to pray. The minute I awoke, I began to pray in tongues until this hellish creature vanished! Hallelujah!

Have you ever noticed that many calamities and deaths occur at night? I once read about a great intercessor from Detroit whom the police recognized for her power in prayer over that city. They even honored her for it. And on Saturday nights, when many people in Detroit were consumed in revelry and drunkenness, this woman would join a group of prayer warriors in intercessory battle against danger. In fact, through her obedience in prayer, she became so effective at preventing danger that whenever the police needed help, they called her prayer group and asked them to help diffuse a potentially dangerous situation.

This woman would take her prayer group over to where the problem was and go into intercession. They had so much success doing this that they even quelled riots and led addicts and drunks to the Lord. They became so effective that the police would even set up a stand on a street for her where they were having problems. The police would then say, "Go to praying, and we'll protect you." Hallelujah!

THE MIGHTY MEN OF GOD PRAYED MUCH

In the days of the mighty evangelist William Booth, the power of God was so great during his meetings that people were literally picked up and transported to the altar to be saved. They didn't even know how they got there. Of course, the Holy Spirit moved them, but they didn't realize this until after it was over. I believe the fervent prayers of the righteous brought this about.

You see, we must not be content with just small moves of God. When we receive these little stirrings, we get so thrilled. But that should just be a signal to us to draw even closer to God in prayer until more moves, stirrings, and miracles come!

You must keep striving to know even more of God. But don't misunderstand me. You never get to the place where you have "arrived" in God. Paul said,

> **Brethren, I count not myself to have apprehended: but this one thing I do, forgetting those things which are behind, and reaching forth unto those things which are before, I press toward the mark for the prize of the high calling of God in Christ Jesus.**
>
> **Philippians 3:13,14**

Look at the life of the prophet Isaiah. He was the "aristocrat" of the prophets. He prophesied and gave words of knowledge to kings. He once prayed, "Oh that thou wouldest rend the heavens, that thou wouldest come down, that the mountains might flow down at thy presence, as when the melting fire burneth, the fire causeth the waters to boil, to make thy name known to thine adversaries, that the nations may tremble at thy presence!" (Isa. 64:1,2).

Isaiah used images that evoked deeper meanings. For example, mountains are symbols of power in this passage. And the boiling waters refer to a spiritual cleansing. Boiling waters kill harmful bacteria and cleanse the water. Well, in the same way, fervent prayers can become so boiling hot that they destroy all harmful works of the devil.

In the book of Revelation, Jesus said to the church in Laodicea, "So then because thou art lukewarm, and neither cold nor hot, I will spew thee out of my mouth" (Rev. 3:16). The word hot here holds the same meaning as the word *fervent*.[1]

Fervent prayers are prayers of love and passion in Christ, flowing out to Him for others. Fervent prayers are so spiritually "hot" that no thermometer in the world can measure their intensity.

You see, hell's fires were lit in the hearts of man after Adam sinned. So it is in the hearts of man that hell's fires must be quenched. Thank God the effectual, fervent prayers of righteous men will quench the fires of hell in people's hearts.

Now, Satan has lit many fires. He has lit the fires of drugs and alcohol that literally drain the youth of this nation. But the church needs to stand by those same words of Isaiah 64:1,2.

Through prayer we remain in continual contact with God. It is we, not God, who must create the right atmosphere for heaven's work on the earth. We must bring God to the people.

So often we want someone else to bring God's presence into a certain place. But every one of us is a divine repository of God's presence. God is a melting and consuming fire! And when we have been in His presence, something should emanate from us that attracts people. People should not need to be begged, wheedled, or cajoled to come to God. Rather, they should cry out, "What must we do to be saved?"

Our prayers should reflect Isaiah's heart cry:

> **When thou didst terrible things which we looked not for, thou camest down, the mountains flowed down at thy presence. For since the beginning of the world men have not heard, nor perceived by the ear, neither hath the eye seen, O God, beside thee, what he hath prepared for him that waiteth for him. Thou meetest him that rejoiceth and worketh righteousness, those that remember thee in thy ways: behold, thou art wroth; for we have sinned: in those is continuance, and we shall be saved.**
>
> **But we are all as an unclean thing, and all our righteousnesses are as filthy rags; and we all do fade as a leaf; and our iniquities, like the wind, have taken us away. And there is none that calleth upon thy name, that stirreth up himself to take hold of thee: for thou hast hid**

thy face from us, and bast consumed us, because of our iniquities.

Isaiah 64:3-7

As I have mentioned before, Israel's sin was that of not praying. Even though they met all the requirements of the law and had all of God's promises, they did not exercise the right, privilege, and function of prayer. Therefore, they suffered the consequences. But it didn't have to be that way. They could have enjoyed the manifestation of God's promises if they had come to Him in prayer.

Remember that when you come to God, you are coming to the most powerful Being in the universe. And when He begins to use His power against your problems, they must do one of two things: bend or break.

PRAYER IS THE GREATEST CHANNEL OF POWER

Prayer is a channel by which one can reach the most powerful listening audience—God. Therefore, when you set out to pray and believe to see God's promises fulfilled, don't give up! You're getting in touch with the power of God, so don't let obstacles turn you back.

David said, "I have pursued mine enemies, and destroyed them; and turned not again until I had consumed them" (2 Sam. 22:38). The Bible says, "If thou faint in the day of adversity, thy strength is small" (Prov. 24:10).

When the enemy tries to discourage you, don't let him. Instead, be encouraged to do what Nehemiah did after his city, Jerusalem, was destroyed. He returned to Jerusalem to rebuild the wall. His writings indicate that he came against the enemy with prayer. Nehemiah said, "Nevertheless we made our prayer unto our God, and set a watch against them day and night, because of them" (Neh. 4:9).

If you want to prevent your enemies from overtaking you, then you too must remember to pray as a watchman on the wall. And as an heir of the new covenant, you have the added power of praying in the Spirit. The Bible says, "And if ye go to war in your land against the enemy that oppresseth you, then ye shall blow an alarm with the trumpets; and ye shall be remembered before the Lord your God, and ye shall be saved from your enemies" (Num. 10:9). That is a picture of praying in the Spirit. Praying in the Spirit is one of the strongest weapons you can use against the enemy.

God told His people to blow an alarm with trumpets when they went to war. Well, what is your trumpet? It is your voice, of course. And you must use it! Lift up your voice in the Spirit, and your doubts, fears, and discouragement will be left behind.

THE GREAT OPPORTUNITY TO COME TO THE THRONE OF GRACE

As people of God, we have been afforded the greatest opportunity ever offered, and that is to come boldly to the throne of grace in times of need. (Heb. 4:16.) We can talk to Jesus there, leaving all our problems at the brazen altar in the outer court, where Jesus Himself took our sin, sickness, disease, and poverty and restored all the things Satan took away from us.

When we come into God's presence in the Spirit, our standing is secure. That is why it is important to picture ourselves standing in the very presence of God when we pray in the Spirit. We do this as an act of our faith.

Through prayer, the compassion of Jesus flows to meet His people's needs and to break the power of sin and Satan over people who seek deliverance. Jesus has vested the authority and power in His people through prayer to break chains of bondage.

Jesus broke the chains of hell, and all you need to do is enforce His victory. Since Jesus paid such a high price to break your chains of bondage, you must never go back—in thought or in deed—to the sin that once enslaved you. As a free person, you must walk and live in His liberty.

The power of God will be just as great tomorrow as it is today. The life that is produced by the Holy Spirit must be maintained by constant communion, or communication, with God and by receiving from Him the resurrection power and life which Jesus purchased for us. By walking with God and communicating with Him in prayer, we learn how to allow Him to flow through us to others.

We can never touch men until we know how to touch God. We must work together with God to maintain His power and anointing in our lives. Let your desire be like that of Paul who said, "Yet indeed I also count all things loss for the excellence of the knowledge of Christ Jesus my Lord, for whom I have suffered the loss of all things, and count them as rubbish, that I may gain Christ" (Phil. 3:8 NKJV).

In order to be useful and pliable in the Master's hands, you must yield to Him. Know that God is urging you to lift up your voice like a trumpet to enforce His great victory in the earth!

CHAPTER SIX

FASTING AND HIDING AWAY WITH GOD

Fasting before God is one of the great secrets to a rich life full of fruitful intercession. During a fast, the appetites of the flesh are put aside and the spirit becomes more sensitive to hear God's voice. This can be a vital practice as you intercede on behalf of others according to God's will.

Throughout biblical history, especially in the Old Testament, people fasted for several different reasons. During times of sorrow, mourning, and great affliction, people would fast to express their grief. Under the law, only one official day was set aside for fasting—the Day of Atonement, which the Israelites observed as an occasion of mourning.

In the New Testament, Jesus gave the church no definite pattern for fasting, perhaps because He didn't want it to become a formula to follow. But He did give us some teaching on this subject. Jesus said that fasting was something to be done at various times for various occasions. And He gave instruction for the manner in which one fasts. In Matthew, He said it was necessary to fast with the correct motives, not as a hypocrite would fast. (Matt. 6:16.)

Jesus insisted that fasting must be done in sincerity and in truth. He said, "Moreover when ye fast, be not, as the hypocrites, of a sad countenance: for they disfigure their faces, that they may appear unto men to fast. Verily I say unto you, They have their reward" (Matt. 6:16).

A hypocrite is someone who deceitfully plays a part well.

The hypocrite only puts on an act. That is where the word comes from.1 A hypocrite is someone who plays several roles well, but with ulterior motives. Unfortunately, some Christians fit this description. These "Christians" attend church and act very pious, but in fact they are hiding a life of sin. It is dangerous to play a role!

You see, fasting doesn't only involve abstaining from food. It is a lifestyle of abstinence from certain carnal pleasures that would take your time and thoughts away from God. Therefore, when we truly fast, we don't touch anything that would distract us from a consecrated prayer life.

THE PURPOSE OF FASTING IS TO DRAW NEAR TO GOD

Jesus demanded that when we seek God by fasting, we should not do so as the hypocrites do. We should not wear a sad countenance and make a big issue of our fasting. Jesus doesn't want us to broadcast the fact that we are fasting.

When we fast, we are not fasting to gain the approval of men; we are fasting for God! The purpose of fasting is to draw near to almighty God and to bring Him into our midst so that *He* can draw others into His presence. Fasting should always glorify God, not man.

Those who fast to be seen by men may get the acclaim of men—the very thing they want. Jesus said about those people, "They have their reward" (v. 16). But those are not the followers Jesus wants. He doesn't want people who are fasting to look as though they are fasting. Fasting should never be an act of hardship, but rather an act of joy. Jesus said, "Appear not unto men to fast, but unto thy Father which is in secret: and thy Father, which seeth in secret, shall reward thee openly" (v. 18).

One of the occasions for a fast mentioned in the Old Testament was the total defeat of the Israelites at Ai. (Josh. 7:4.) After this defeat, Joshua and his people fell down before the ark of God, where His presence dwelt. For an entire day, they remained upon their faces before the ark of God, seeking the reason for their defeat. As they fasted, God revealed to them the reason they were defeated so badly: hidden sin was in their camp. (v. 11.) That incident was the only recorded time that Joshua fasted. The entire book of Joshua is one of conquest. But when the children of Israel didn't conquer the enemy as God had promised, they were compelled to get on their faces before God and. fast in order to receive God's direction.

The Old Testament provides another example of fasting in the life of David. David fasted when Bathsheba's and his baby became very sick. As long as the baby was sick, David fasted as a way of mourning. However, when the child died, David arose from his prostrate position, washed himself, and returned to his normal life, laying aside his grief.

In fact, throughout the Old Testament, people fasted as a form of mourning over a loss. Fasting was not observed to try to change God or force Him to move His hand. That is not the purpose of fasting. The purpose for fasting is to become more consecrated and sensitive to God.

Jesus' contemporaries questioned Him about His fasting habits. The scribes and the Pharisees complained, "Why don't Your disciples fast as the Pharisees do?" (Luke 5:33.) Jesus answered them wisely, saying, "Can ye make the children of the bridechamber fast, while the bridegroom is with them? But the days will come, when the bridegroom shall be taken away from them, and then shall they fast in those days" (Luke 5:34,35).

JESUS FASTED TO PASS THE TEST THAT ADAM AND ISRAEL FAILED

As I mentioned before, Jesus didn't set any particular pattern for fasting. He didn't say, for example, that you must fast on a certain day of the week or during

151

a certain time of the day. He left it up to the Holy Spirit to impress people when to fast.

However, when Jesus was taken into the wilderness to be tempted by the devil for forty days, He fasted the entire time. (Matt. 4:1,2.) Do you know why He fasted forty days and forty nights? The answer is that forty is a probationary number. The number "forty" belonged to the people of Israel, who had wandered forty years in the wilderness as punishment for their unbelief. An entire generation of Israelites had failed God's tests. Therefore, the reason Jesus had to fast forty days and forty nights in the wilderness was that He had to pass God's testing of His character in the wilderness.

Jesus set the standard. Jesus fulfilled God's requirements by the power of the Holy Spirit. He did not do it by the power of His flesh. That is why the rest of us cannot fulfill God's requirements in the flesh either. Jesus fulfilled God's requirements by praying and fasting. He lived on earth as a man who had the full anointing of the Holy Spirit.

God required Jesus to pass the tests that Adam, Israel, and all of mankind had failed. Jesus had to live a life without sin, and He did just that. He passed the test for us. He conquered the enemy and went on to victory.

He came out of the wilderness for the launching of His public ministry.

Jesus never said, "You must fast forty days as I did." No, He left that up to us. He simply showed us by example how to live to please the Father.

GOD WILL CALL YOU TO HIDE AWAY WITH HIM FOR A SEASON

There are times when God will call you to hide away with Him in the Spirit for a season. During these times, He wants you to withdraw from certain things so He can impart His wisdom into your spirit. Usually, the Lord will do a new work in you when He asks you to withdraw. However, this doesn't mean God wants you to cut yourself off from your family or your job. But He may call you to set aside some of your outside pursuits so you can seek His face and develop a deeper relationship with Him.

When God told me emergency hours would be coming up in the world that would require urgent prayer, He told me I was to hide myself away to prepare for these times. And for four years, I was not to teach or preach in public. I was to hide myself away with Him in prayer until I heard the word of the Lord saying, *Go back to public ministry.*

There are examples of this in the Word. In 1 Kings, for example, God outlines His divine order and direction for calling Elijah apart from others: "And the word of the Lord came unto him, saying, Get thee hence, and turn thee eastward, and hide thyself by the brook Cherith, that is before Jordan" (1 Kings 17:2,3).

God knew there would be a famine in the land where Elijah lived, but God made provision for him. In fact, God wanted Elijah hidden away so securely that He sent birds to take food to Elijah. After that season of preparation, God released him to go into ministry.

You see, preparation time is never wasted. God will never ask you to separate yourself from others for a season without a reason. When He calls you to come away with Him, that means He wants to impart something to you. And usually, it is something that will bless others.

Look at the ministry of John the Baptist. God called him into the desert to hide away with Him. John remained in the wilderness until it was time for him to announce the coming of the Messiah. (Luke 1:80.) At that time, John left the desert, where he had been hidden away with God, and went back to the banks of the river Jordan. There he preached repentance to Israel, and the people eagerly came to hear him preach in his wilderness pulpit. (Matt. 3:1-5.)

John's ministry was to prepare Israel for the Messiah's coming. In the same way, God may call you to come away with Him to prepare for future events. When He does this, God is not asking you to abandon your family or forget your responsibilities. He may ask you to set aside some of your social functions or entertainment time to be with Him so that He can impart something special to you.

WHEN GOD HIDES YOU AWAY, HE IS PREPARING YOU FOR A NEW WORK

Do you know why God is calling the church to prayer in this hour as never before? It is because the Messiah is returning! Jesus will reappear for His bride, but it will take prayer to prepare the way.

When Jesus traveled back to His hometown and sat down in the synagogue, He sat in the chair left vacant for the Messiah to read the Scripture prophesying His coming. For that, the Jews wanted to kill Him. They knew the man who sat in that seat was to be the Messiah. They believed Jesus had blasphemed God, because they did not believe Jesus was the Messiah since He had grown up among them.

But by revealing Himself in this way, Jesus was showing people that the thirty-year preparation period had ended and the day of His revelation to Israel was at hand. On that day, He broke His connection with His earthly parents, went to the Jordan for His baptism, and became subject only to His Father in heaven. Then He was able to begin His public ministry. But notice that for the previous thirty years, Jesus had been hidden away in preparation before He appeared in public ministry.

God values preparation time. Preparation time is never wasted. All the great ministers of faith in the Bible took time to prepare before entering full-time ministry. Paul did not immediately launch out into ministry after he became a believer. Instead, he was led to Arabia, where God gave him great revelation and illumination in the Word of the living God. (Gal. 1:17,18.) Only after this preparation time did Paul begin his ministry.

NO TURNING BACK IN PRAYER

Prayer will compel people and nations to make decisions either for or against God. When we pray for people, they must make the decision to either stay where they are or to go on with God. God is a God who moves. Genesis 1:2 says, "The Spirit of God moved..." and He has been moving onward ever since. For example, in the Bible, He always told His people, "Go forward! Don't ever go back. Go on to perfection." (Mt. 5:48; Heb. 6:1.)

Daniel was greatly beloved of God, and he was able to perceive the signs of the times. He knew that it was not God's will for His people to be where they were. And he knew when it was time for them to come into the promises of God. So, he set himself to seek God in prayer on the matter. His prayers forced people to make a decision to either continue in captivity or to seek freedom.

That is why there is such a great need for intercession today: It will bring men and women to an ultimate decision point for God.

God speaks of multitudes of people in the valley of decision. In fact, this is that hour to make a great decision for God! This is the time to decide whether to move forward with God or not. God is not a God of stagnation.

GOD WILL HIDE HIS PEOPLE AWAY IN TIMES OF PERIL

God tells us that He will hide His people away in Him during times of peril. Isaiah 26:20 says, "Come, my people, enter thou into thy chambers, and shut thy doors about thee." The "chambers" were places within the temple in which the treasures of God were kept. God keeps His treasures hidden away.

God's people are also His treasures, and He hides them away during times of peril. He spoke to Noah before the flood came and told him and his household to enter the ark of safety. Therefore, Noah and his household were spared. (Gen. 6,7.)

Noah's generation had heard him preach that a flood was coming, but when the rains began, only those who had listened were spared. Noah and his family went into the ark (Gen. 7:5), and God—not man—shut the door.

That is why God says, "Come, my people, enter thou into thy chambers, and shut thy doors about thee" (Isa.

26:20). This is a call to the church, because the church is preparing for the return of Jesus! Hallelujah!

The Bible says, "Behold, the Lord cometh out of his place" (Isa. 26:21). The Lord's place is at the right hand of the Father. That is where we are too! I have already been translated by faith into a position of authority with Jesus. My body is just awaiting the great metamorphosis, when it will join my spirit in that marvelous and beautiful transformation! That experience will be indescribable!

Before long the veil of our flesh will be lifted, and old habits will no longer dominate our minds. We will experience such marvelous freedom when that veil is removed! Hallelujah! We will be able to see with clarity as never before.

Again, the Bible says, "Behold, the Lord cometh out of His place" (Isa. 26:21). He is coming out of His place to do something. And it will be something good for those who keep His commandments. He will not punish those who love Him-who truly love Him and are not living after the flesh. In fact, He will reward those who truly love Him. But there *will* come a time when God must judge the sinners. Isaiah 26:21 continues, "Behold, the Lord cometh out of his place to punish the inhabitants of the earth for their iniquity: the earth also shall disclose her blood, and shall no more cover her slain."

Sometimes people just read the Bible as if it only contained historical information, with no practical application for us today. But all Scripture was given by inspiration of God, and it applies to every age. The Holy Spirit was, is, and will always be the same throughout history. (Heb. 13:8.)

Those who hide themselves away in the Lord have nothing to fear. God assures His people of this: "And they shall be mine, saith the Lord of hosts, in that day when I make up my jewels; and I will spare them, as a man spareth his own son that serveth him" (Mal. 3:17).

Once when I visited England, I saw the crown jewels of the monarchs. Many guards watched over them. I believe that if men set up guards to watch over their earthly jewels, how much more is there a heavenly guard set up to protect you and me. You and I are the jewels that will adorn the Master's crown. Through us, God will display His victory over Satan and His glorious rule of the entire world.

God doesn't care about natural jewels, such as diamonds, rubies, or emeralds. They are mere stones to Him. God's crown will be made up of living stones-you and I will be His crown of glory. He will display us as a light that will shine upon the world! Hallelujah!

God does hide us away for a season sometimes. But He only does so to perfect the treasures He has placed within us. After crafting us in secret, God will then bring us out in His glory to shine upon the earth.

During the years I spent hiding away in intercession, God told me that the time would come when people would physically see the glory of the Lord. Those who stood before large crowds would become so filled with the brilliance of God's light that crowds would actually be blinded by the brightness!

Let me tell you about a true story that illustrates the idea of hiding away in prayer with God. I fell one time and broke the patella bone of my left leg, crushing the knee. Of course, it was very painful, and I was incapacitated for some time. My doctor, who was a very kind, Jewish man, told me that my knee would need to be totally rebuilt.

He said to me, "Mrs. Wilkerson, what do you want to do? Do you want me to totally rebuild this knee? Because I don't think anything else will do."

"No, doctor," I said. "I don't want you to totally rebuild my knee. I will trust God for my healing. My God is the same as yours, so I will trust Him to heal me."

"All right," he said. "I'll give you twelve days to make up your mind. Healing never sets in before two weeks anyway, so that time won't make any difference. And if after two weeks you want your knee to be rebuilt, you can come back and let me know."

So he gave me twelve days to decide what to do. I had to choose to either have my knee operated on or to trust God for a miraculous healing. Well, during that twelve days I hid myself away with God, praying in faith in God and His Word for my healing.

At the end of twelve days, I went back to the doctor.

"What is your decision?" he asked me.

I said, "I haven't changed. I'm going the same route I said I would. I will trust my God to heal me."

"All right," he said. "Meet me at the hospital in the morning, and we'll put a cast and a brace on your leg."

Well, I was put in a cast from the top of my leg down to my foot. And the doctor said I would probably be that way for eight weeks.

I hated it. It was like being in prison. My leg would swell up inside that cast and cause all kinds of discomfort. Finally, I said to my husband, "Get a hacksaw and a screwdriver! I am tired of this thing." And we split that cast right off of my leg!

When I went back to the doctor, I asked him, "How do you like this?"

He took one look at my leg without the cast and said, "I don't blame you. I would have done the same thing myself." Bless his heart. Medically, he is rated as one of the top doctors in his field. But he was so kind to me. He didn't look upon me with contempt for what I did.

Instead he put me in a new cast that was less constricting and sent me on my way to believe for my healing. Again, I hid myself away with God. I got close to God, prayed, and believed for my healing for five weeks.

When I went back to see my doctor for my final checkup, he took X-rays and was amazed at what he saw. He said, "Mrs. Wilkerson, you made the right decision. God has healed you. I couldn't have done that good of a job myself. Only your God could have built a new knee like that!" Praise God! God totally re-created my knee.

But after I got out of the cast, I thought I would just walk right out of there and go home with no problems at all. But I was wrong!

After five weeks my leg began to have painful muscle spasms because it had been stiff and immobile for so long. The muscle spasms became so strong that they began to affect other nerves and muscles in my back. I found myself in pain the likes of which I had never experienced before in my life. There were days that I literally felt like I was on fire. At times I would cry out to God, "Father, if my ministry is finished, if You're through with me, please let me go home."

Although I have to admit I was in pain, I continued to say, "Satan, I'm going on to healing! You will not hold me back. I'm going on in Jesus' name!" I had to wrestle for my healing. I knew it was already mine, but I had to fight the symptoms of pain the devil was trying to use to tell me otherwise.

One day, after having only slightly recovered from the pain, I went to Brother Kenneth Hagin Sr.'s seminar where he gave me a word from the Lord. Now, Bro. Hagin didn't know all the negative confessions I'd been speaking about wanting to go home to be with Jesus.

Bro. Hagin said, "Mrs. Wilkerson, you are never again to say you want to go home to heaven! God isn't through with you. You're going back to a great ministry. In fact, you will see things you have never seen in the history of your ministry."

THE VISITATION OF AN ANGELIC HORSE

Maybe I had to continue to fight the symptoms of pain, but I had won my healing the minute I prayed.

Do you know what it means to wrestle with principalities, powers, and the rulers of the darkness of this world? (Eph. 6:12.) That word "wrestle" means to intensely combat.[2] Someone once said that we could write over a lot of church sanctuaries, "We wrestle not." Well, I learned many years ago that prayer is intense combat. I learned that I was battling against principalities, powers, and rulers of the darkness of this world who would love to destroy me. They wanted to cripple and maim me, and they would have, but God protected me.

God came to me one day after I was so exhausted from praying, battling in the Spirit, and warring with my Sword, the Word of God. I had battled until I was completely exhausted, and I said, "God, I can't go any further."

I remember when it happened. At nine o'clock that night I was sitting in my chair, crying out to God, when all of a sudden I was caught up into the spirit realm. I became so God-conscious that I was no longer self-conscious or world-conscious at all. I even lost consciousness of the terrible pain I was in. And in a vision, I saw a beautiful white horse with a rider come into my yard. It trotted up my driveway and stepped onto my patio. I remember thinking as I sat there, *Why is this horse coming to me like this?* Then that horse came right through my glass doors and into my house!

You see, spirit beings can pass through anything. After Jesus' resurrection, He appeared in a room without even coming through a door. (John 20:19.) Life in the spirit realm is very different from life in the natural realm.

Well, that beautiful white horse and rider came right into my living room and stood by my chair. The Holy Spirit let me know this was an angelic horse I was to ride during times of battle. The Holy Spirit told me, *This being is a warrior angel from heaven sent to help you in this battle. You have been battling principalities, powers, and the rulers of darkness of this world who would love to destroy you. But I have prayed for you that your faith fail not.*

I didn't know it at the time, but I had friends who happened to be in London, England, praying for me. Later when they called, they asked, "What happened to you at nine o'clock on this night?" Well, I compared notes with them and found that they had been interceding for me at the very time I was at my wit's end, crying out to God, saying, "God, I can't go any further."

Meanwhile, as my friends prayed, this angelic horse kept guard over me. I had seen it as clearly as I see things in the natural.

When I had finally come out of the vision, I looked at my husband and asked, "Did you see anything just then?"

"No," he replied.

But all during that night as I closed my eyes, I could see that white horse and rider. They were patrolling my surroundings and watching over me. Sometimes they would leave the bedroom, and I'd see them go right through the wall outside as if to patrol the yard. Then they would come back through the wall and patrol my bedroom.

God reminded me again, *This is one of heaven's warring angels. He has been sent to recruit help for you in this battle.*

I went to church the next day, and while we were driving I looked out the window and saw that white horse and rider following me.

Isn't God good? He sent help just in the nick of time! And if He'll do it for me, He'll do it for you.

PRAYER PREVENTS NEEDLESS TRAGEDY

God will always protect His children if they hide away with Him in prayer. Unfortunately, however, many people have not done this.

Adam and Eve didn't consult with God in prayer when the tempter came to them in the Garden of Eden.

If only they had prayed and talked with God before they ate, they would not have been the cause of the proclamation of the curse upon man.

Abraham and Sarah didn't consult God before they decided to bear a child with Hagar. Instead, Abraham listened to the voice of his wife, not the voice of his God. (Gen. 16:1-6.) God had already spoken to Abraham about the promised son, Isaac. (Gen. 15:5.) However, Abraham made a mistake, contributing to the enmity in the Middle East we experience even today.

Saul lost his kingdom partly because he never spent enough time in prayer. He didn't build an altar for prayer as he should have. He depended upon Samuel to do his praying for him, and consequently, Saul lost his kingdom. (1 Sam. 15.) Through the power of prayer he could have been a great and mighty man of God, but he never was.

As you can see, a lack of prayer has dire consequences. Prayer is one of the most powerful weapons we have at our disposal. It is an awesome tool.

GOD COLLECTS TEARS OVER THE ABOMINATIONS OF THE LAND

Psalm 56:8 says, "Put thou my tears into thy bottle: are they not in thy book?" That means that the true tears of believers are filling up a bottle before the golden altar of glory. That golden altar is the altar of prayer. When we approach God in the spirit through prayer, we appear at that golden altar.

God collects your tears when you cry over the abominations in the land, and He records them in His book. (Ps. 56:8.) That means the very hour you call for help, the tide of battle turns in your favor. Of this one thing you can be sure: *God is for you!* And if God is for us, no one can stand against us. (Rom. 8:31.) Isn't that marvelous! The following is a prophecy the Lord gave me about the benefits of prayer. Even though this prophecy was given to me, it can apply to your life too. The same God who gave me this promise also gives it to you.

A WORD FOR THE BODY OF CHRIST

The Holy Spirit says the following to the body of Christ:

> *I have many things to finish in you before that hour comes upon the land. I have many things to give you if you will allow Me to. Therefore, listen to Me and hide thyself from the noise, the din, the chaos, the ruin, and the wreckage of the world. I will show you things to come, and you will know and see things*

vividly. You will even be able to see many things in Technicolor, as it were. I will put double emphasis upon seeing things in the spirit.

I will no longer hide from thee that which I am about to do. If you will obey my Word and hide thyself away with Me, you will never see the indignation that is coming upon the nations of the world.

My preparation of My church for My appearing will be very, very intricate and detailed. You will not draw back any longer. When I reach out to you and My voice comes to you, you will be like My child in the Song of Solomon. When the voice of the bridegroom was heard, they ran after Him. Thus shall it be in this hour—the hour that all the other hours have pointed toward. This is the day that all other days have spoken about. This is the day that all the prophets longed to see but were not able to. This is your day.

CHAPTER SEVEN

PRAYER: OPTION OR NECESSITY?

Throughout the years our intercessory group prayed, God taught us marvelous things. He taught us things I'd never heard anybody teach before. That is why prayer is so important to the Christian walk. It is like the air we breathe. We need it!

Can you live without breathing? Of course not! I often say, "Just try living without air. You'll be on the floor in no time." You can go without food or water longer than you can go without air.

What air is to the body, prayer is to the spirit. By praying, you take in sustenance for your spirit from God.

You're breathing in the very life of God. And the same Holy Spirit that gave birth to your human spirit maintains the life within you. That is why prayer is so vital.

Another reason prayer is so important is that it is our way to communicate with God. When Adam and Eve were shut out of the presence of God and could no longer fellowship with Him face to face, the only avenue of communication with God that was left open to them was the avenue of prayer. Prayer bridged the gap between them and God.

HOW THE WORD AND PRAYER OPERATE TOGETHER

Contained within the Word of God are His instructions for mankind. In other words, God tells His people how to live as He wants them to. But that is not enough.

Once you understand God's plan, then you have to set it into motion, and that is where prayer comes in. God expects you to pray to set His plan in motion. It is not enough to simply have a Bible study. That is wonderful, but you must follow it up with prayer. You must have the Word, but it takes prayer to animate the Word, to make it alive. And it takes prayer to execute

God's plan. It takes the Holy Spirit to live this life within you.

Prayer should be an ongoing practice in your life. Prayer is an eternal work. Did you know that you will even be praying when you go into glory?

The book of Revelation shows us that there is prayer in heaven. "And [the saints in heaven] cried with a loud voice, saying, How long, O Lord, holy and true, dost thou not judge and avenge our blood on them that dwell on the earth?" (Rev. 6:10). The saints in heaven are praying to God for justice. Prayer is an eternal action.

LEARN TO DISCERN BETWEEN THE FLESH AND THE SPIRIT

People have sometimes said things to me that I knew were off the mark. As I would listen with my spiritual ears to what they were saying, I could tell it was wrong. The Holy Spirit inside me always tells me, *This is of the flesh,* or *This is of the Spirit.* In other words, He always alerts me to the truth. But we must exercise our spiritual senses to know the difference between the Spirit and the flesh.

I have sat under some of the greatest leaders in the body of Christ. For example, I sat under Smith Wigglesworth, Howard Carter, and Stanley Frodsham. I have sat under some of the "Gamaliels," or noted Bible teachers, in the kingdom of God. They have taught me how to enter the presence of God to learn His voice.

The great leaders of God will tell you when something is nonsense and frivolous instead of godly and genuine. In a great prophecy I once heard, God called the excesses of fleshly behavior "chaff" instead of the wheat kernels of wisdom. God said the following:

> *I will never bless the chaff. Don't come and offer that to Me, because I don't want it. It doesn't please me; it only pleases your flesh. And if you are not careful, you will bring up a generation who loves nothing but that which pleases the natural senses—not the spirit, but the flesh. And when you begin to draw people out of this excess, taking them over into realms of God, where real life dwells, they will revolt. They will revolt because they would rather have the flesh than the true works of the Holy Spirit.*

THE PITFALL OF COMPLACENCY

In the end times in which we are living, complacency is one of the greatest obstacles to overcome. We can see an example of this in the prophetic message to the church at Laodicea. (Rev. 3:14-22.) This church is known as the one that is lukewarm. In other words, it is complacent.

It is so easy to become complacent—to settle in comfort where you are. Admittedly, sometimes it is easy to think you no longer need to enter into combat against the enemy. But complacency is a dangerous condition in which to be. Jesus said to the one who can overcome this lukewarm condition, "I will grant you to sit with Me on My throne." (Rev. 3:21.)

Satan is crafty. He knows how to deceive people. He knows that when things are going well, people usually take it easy and relax spiritually. When Satan unleashes intense oppression, he knows people will eventually cry out to God. (Ex. 2:23,24; Judg. 6:6,7; Isa. 19:20.)

The Bible says that when everything was going well in Israel, the prayers of the people were only like drops of water instead of a river. It's the same for many of us today. We offer a little drop of prayer every now and then. But when times begin to get rough, people begin to buckle their seat belts and go to their knees in prayer.

You see, Satan is a strategist and he knows how to test the church of the living God. The church must shake off complacency, for a complacent church can never overcome Satan's deception. We must maintain a vigil of prayer and intercession.

I have had to fight complacency in my own life. My husband and I once had an automobile dealership that became very successful. We rose from nothing to having a good business. But the more God blessed us, the more I had to go to the secret place of the Most High and humble my flesh.

My flesh by nature is very proud. In fact, I had been so proud at one point that when I went to the altar to receive Christ, my makeup got messed up so I stopped to check my face on the way. I have never seen anyone else do that. But that is how proud I was.

God told me that when I became a Christian, I must never return to pride or selfishness. He warned me, so I made a commitment to pray to remain humble. The more God has blessed us, the more I have prayed to humble myself. And God has blessed me. God told me what things He would give me through the years. He has been faithful to give me everything He promised!

GOD WANTS TO QUALIFY YOU FOR AN ETERNAL POSITION

It is so important that all of us go to heaven, because God needs us to attend to important business there.

It will be like a meeting of the House of Lords in London. When officials need to make a vital decision that would affect England, they call the House of Lords to a meeting. And any member of the House of Lords who is away must return to attend the meeting.

Well, we're members of the House of *the* Lord! And let me tell you, when He calls a meeting, we have to go. It doesn't matter where we are when the Lord calls. We have to go.

But until then, the church is still ruling and reigning on the earth! She has the authority to do things on God's behalf. One of the reasons she has such a big job is that God wants to show Satan what He can do with a "weaker vessel."

You see, in the Bible, the woman is called "the weaker vessel." (1 Peter 3:7.) But God performed mighty deeds through women. Since the woman is a type of the church, God will do mighty things through her just to show that fallen angel, Satan, what He can do with a "weaker vessel."

Here on earth, the church is learning how to handle things that we will do in heaven. God is qualifying us and preparing us for an eternal position of royalty.

Jeanne Wilkerson around 1930, not long after she married D.B.

Jeanne and D.B. Wilkerson in their home, 1940.

Jeanne at 23 with her son, Tink. Taken around the time of Jeanne's first prophecy experience.

Jeanne, with her interpreter, ministering in Mexico City, 1976.

Jeanne, center left, and Marilyn, far right, ministering on television in the early 1980s. Pastor Billy Joe Daughtery, left.

Jeanne and D.B. Wilkerson with Brother and Mrs. Hagin, May 1980.

Marilyn, D.B., Jeanne, Tink and Diane at D.B. and Jeanne's 50th wedding anniverary celebration, May 1980.

Marilyn singing before Jeanne's sermon, Victory Christain Center, 1983.

Jeanne Wilkerson ministering at Victory Christian Center Word Explosion, August 1983.

Jeanne Wilkerson, 1960s.

Jeanne Wilkerson ministering during her city-wide Bible study, Tulsa, Oklahoma, 1980s.

Jeanne and D.B. Wilkerson, Colorado Springs, Colorado, 1978.

CHAPTER EIGHT

THE PRIESTLY ROLE OF THE BELIEVER

The book of Luke describes to us the prayer life of a King. The Jews who testified against Jesus at His trial asked Him if He was the King of the Jews—the Messiah. (Luke 23:3.) Of course, we know He is the King of kings, and since we are heirs of His kingdom, we have also become royalty.

We are New Testament kings and priests. (Rev. 1:6; 5:10.) In the Bible, the ministries of kings, priests, and prophets are closely linked together. These were the three primary ministries of the Old Testament.

You are a royal priest, but without a solid prayer life, you will never be able to reign. As a priest, you have access into the presence of God to pray for others. You have the authority to call life or death for individuals. First John 5:16 says that if you see your brother commit a sin that is not unto death, you can ask God for mercy for that person, and He will give him life. As a priest, through prayer you are able to grant life to a brother who has erred. But prayer is the only way you can do it. If you never use your authority to ask anything of God, you will never accomplish anything.

The word *ask* is a significant word. It doesn't just mean to casually say, "Would you give me something?" The act of asking in prayer means to link up with God in divine communion and become so one with Him that your will becomes one with His.

When we ask things of God, we become His voice in this generation. When we are so motivated, moved and animated by the Holy Spirit, we will speak the *rhema* of God in partnership with God, and it will come to pass. There is a vast difference between speaking forth God's Word in faith and just parroting it. To speak it in faith, we must be in partnership with God.

EARLY CHURCH PATTERNS OF PRAYER

Just after Christ's resurrection, the early church never knew what would happen next. But eventually patterns were established, and church services began to be held. The early church held divinely ordained prayer meetings, much like we need to hold in these last days.

Prayer is the only way to monitor the workings of the Holy Spirit. We should test everything to discern whether it is from God or not. For example, I read about a gentleman who was so spiritually in tune that he could immediately detect whether or not a move of the Spirit upon an individual in a service was genuine. He would tell the person yielding to the Holy Spirit to continue if it was truly valid. However, if the work was not from God, he would tell the person to be seated.

God monitors His work. He knows what comes from His own Being, what is of the Holy Spirit and what is not. No one can fool the Holy Spirit. He knows both our hearts and His own work.

You might ask, "How can we tell whether something is from God or not?" I would respond, "Don't you know your own children? Don't you know your own works?" Certainly you do! Likewise, the Holy Spirit knows His works. He knows whether or not a work is emanating

185

from Himself. Furthermore, as God's children, we should know the source of our works too.

We need wisdom for this sort of discernment. If there is one thing I desire above all things, it is wisdom. I want to know how to operate effectively and efficiently in the Spirit. I want to be skilled in the things of God.

The Bible says that even the musicians were trained and skilled. That meant the Holy Spirit trained them. (2 Chron. 34:12.) When I was younger, I trained to sing the blues, jazz, and other types of contemporary music, but I wasn't trained to sing Christian songs and hymns. Naturally, when I became a Christian, I wanted to learn to sing those songs. So I told the Holy Spirit, "You are the best teacher to train me to sing Your songs." Well, He taught me, and eventually I became very skilled in singing those songs.

THE PRIESTLY ROLE OF THE BELIEVER IS TO MINISTER LIFE

When Adam sinned in the Garden of Eden, he brought death into the earth. It was necessary that God build an altar and use a sacrifice to cover Adam's sin. Ever since that time, it has been necessary for someone to mediate between God and man so that God's wrath would not fall on sinners.

As you know, the Old Testament requirements of the law remained in place until Jesus came to be the sacrifice on that great altar called Calvary. God built that altar—not man. God also provided the offering, His only Son, Jesus, who was not only the High Priest, but also the Mediator between God and man.

Notice what the Bible says about the life and ministry of Jesus:

> **So also Christ glorified not himself to be made an high priest; but he that said unto him, Thou art my Son, to day have I begotten thee. As he saith also in another place, Thou art a priest for ever after the order of Melchisedec. Who in the days of his flesh, when he had offered up prayers and supplications with strong crying and tears unto him that was able to save him from death, and was heard in that he feared; though he were a Son, yet learned he obedience by the things which he suffered.**
>
> **Hebrews 5:5-8**

Jesus came to earth to minister spiritual life where there was none. He lived on earth as a man totally dependent on the Father. He maintained an avid spiritual life by staying connected to the Father.

Therefore, He was always a victor over the temptations and attacks of the enemy.

Although He remained dependent upon the Father for His authority, He was totally human. He suffered human weaknesses, just as we do. However, the Holy Spirit strengthened Him and enabled Him to complete His ministry on earth. The Holy Spirit will do the same thing for us, if we will follow Jesus' example of dependence upon the Father. If Jesus had once acted independently of the Father, in that moment Satan would have gained the advantage, and Jesus would have become the *second* fallen Adam. But Jesus resisted temptation. Notice what the Bible says about Jesus' suffering:

> **Who in the days of his flesh, when he had offered up prayers and supplications with strong crying and tears unto him that was able to save him from death, and was heard in that he feared; though he were a Son, yet learned he obedience by the things which he suffered.**
>
> **Hebrews 5:7,8**

Jesus was obedient to the Father. He could have said, "I'm the Son of God. I'm born of a virgin, filled with the Spirit, and I don't need to pray." But He didn't. In fact, Pilate asked Jesus, "Art thou the King of the Jews?" And Jesus answered, "Thou sayest it" (Luke 23:3).

Jesus was born to minister life to others. And He did so through a life of dependence on the Father. Although He had to first die to bring life, He made the ultimate sacrifice and showed the way of salvation to those who would follow.

PRIVATE PRAYER PRODUCES THE PUBLIC FRUIT OF MINISTRY

Sometimes we may get the idea that we don't need to pray. But that is simply not true. If Jesus needed to pray, how much more do we need to? The only reason He was able to resist sin was that He was obedient to the call of the Holy Spirit on His life. He prayed constantly before He fulfilled His ministry, and if we are going to pattern our lives after His, we have to spend time in prayer too.

Let me tell you about a man under whose teaching I sat years ago. He lived in a foreign country and had such influence there that even the ruler of the country came knocking at his door. This man had favor!

Years later, I was in a seminar talking to another gentleman who had been a missionary in the country this man had lived in for many years. I asked the man at the seminar what had happened to this highly influential man. I could hardly believe what I heard. He told me, "Mrs. Wilkerson, he wound up on the streets of New York City as a drunk."

"Oh, no!" I exclaimed. "What happened?"

"He thought that because he had a mighty touch from God, it would always be there," the man at the seminar explained.

Sadly, some of us get so used to riding on the crest of the wave of God's anointing that we forget it is a *gift* given by the inspiration of God. We sometimes forget that it is an honor and privilege just to breathe it in through prayer and the power of the Holy Spirit.

God has showed me that it is very dangerous to let your public works overrule a private devotional life with God. It is just like an old saying I once heard: "Seven days without prayer makes one weak." And that is the truth!

The Scriptures say that Jesus often left the multitudes to withdraw into the mountains and spend nights communing with the Father. Afterward, He would come down from the mountain into the valley to minister life to the multitudes. After spending time with the Father, He would be pregnant with God's life from spending time in His presence. (Matt. 14:23; Mark 6:46; Luke 9:28; John 6:15.)

Moses did the same thing. He went up a mountain and into the presence of God for forty days and nights. And there He became so saturated with God's presence that God's glory overshadowed both that mountain and Moses' countenance. When Moses descended, His face shone with the radiance of divine life. (Ex. 34:29-35.)

PRAYING GIVES BIRTH TO CHILDREN IN THE NATURAL AND IN THE SPIRIT

A careful study of the ministry of the Levitical priesthood reveals a type of the ministry of Jesus. The Levitical priest was the one who mediated between God and man and ministered at the altar of God. (Ex. 28.)

An example of the spirit of a true priest can be found in a story in the book of Genesis. The heart's cry of a young woman named Rachel who was yearning to bear children touched the heart of God. Rachel was the beloved wife of Jacob, and it was for the love of Rachel that Jacob labored a total of fourteen years under the hand of Laban. (Gen. 29.) But after their marriage, the Bible says, "And when Rachel saw that she bare Jacob no children, Rachel envied her sister; and said unto Jacob, Give me children, or else I die" (Gen. 30:1).

In those days, the inability to bear children was one of the greatest reproaches that could come upon a woman. But in the spiritual realm, it is also one of the greatest reproaches that can come upon the church. The church must bear spiritual children.

Rachel was barren in the natural. This is a type of the human spirit. The human spirit is barren spiritually until it is reborn. However, once the human spirit has experienced a touch of divine life, it will produce the life of God.

In the natural, if a woman can't bear children, she will be part of a dying generation. Well, it is the same way with the church. Churches that are saving the lost are blessed: They are bearing children. But the churches that don't produce spiritual offspring are dying off.

Therefore, don't ever let the travailing that brings forth sons and daughters in the spirit cease among you. It is when Zion travails that sons and daughters will be born again.

We know that when people are born into this world, they must be born again; otherwise, they will die spiritually. God says to the church, *I will let you become a partner with Me to enter into travail in the Spirit so that we may bring children conceived in iniquity and born in sin, out from the clutches of hell.* This task will take the power of intercession among believers by the Holy Spirit to bring sinners into the family of God.

Sometimes parents come to me and say, "Pray for my children." When this happens I usually say, "Do you pray for them yourself? Have you poured yourself out in intercession before God to break those yokes of bondage? Because if you haven't, then don't ask anyone else to pray for your children until you pray first."

You see, we're always trying to get someone else to pour themselves out in prayer for us and for our children. But I never ask others to pour themselves out for mine. I have poured myself out in prayer for my own children.

Do you know that originally every man was supposed to be a priest in his own family? It's true. According to the divine order of God, every man would have been a priest in his own home, winning his own people to God. Therefore, we would never need a preacher. The man of the family would automatically become a priest unto God. (Gen. 8:20,21; Ex. 12:3-7; Judg. 18:19; Job 1:5; 42:8-10; 1 Peter 2:5,9.)

We know that because of disobedience, not every family has a priest unto God in the home. But in God's initial plan, we wouldn't need to come together and travail to win our children back to the Lord, breaking the yoke of hell off them. We would just break it off by the power of God and train them up in the way they ought to go. (Prov. 22:6.)

If every man were priest of his own home, we would all come together as families for the great celebration in heaven. That was God's original plan for families. But God has provided a backup plan, and we can still be together in heaven. Hallelujah!

The Bible describes the treasures in heaven for those who will seek them. The prophet Ezekiel had a vision of the millennial temple, which will face the north. God said, "And the chamber whose prospect is toward the north is for the priests, the keepers of the charge of the altar...which come near to the Lord to minister unto him" (Eze. 40:46).

Precious treasures were kept in the chambers of the priest in the Old Testament. They were treasures that had been imported from all over the world. Some of them had even come from Solomon's ships that sailed to all the major ports of the known world. When the treasure was brought back to the temple, the priests had access to it.

This is another picture of the believer-priest who is invited to enter, through prayer and by faith, into the great storehouses of God to bring down treasure from heaven. Through the prayers of priests, heaven's treasures manifest here on earth. (Deut. 28:12.)

There are treasures in heaven that no man has yet touched or made visible to the natural world. But God is waiting for faith to rise in our hearts to enter into those chambers by way of the golden altar of incense. He wants us, His priests, to bring out those hidden treasures for the world to see.

Some of them have never even been claimed. They are still there waiting for some individual to enter by way of the golden altar by faith. God wants His treasures brought down to earth so He can display them to the world. The status quo of what has been demonstrated on earth is not enough. We must reach higher for the treasures of heaven.

The ministry of a priest is the same power made available to the believer-priest today: to bring life out of death. That is why it is so important to maintain your own spiritual life within. Only when we have strong, overflowing spirits ourselves can we give life to others. As Peter said, "Such as I have give I thee" (Acts 3:6).

Do you remember the story of the Shunamite woman who went to the prophet Elisha after her son died? She saddled a donkey and rode to find the man of God. Upon finding the prophet on Mount Carmel, she fell at his feet.

Her life gives us a picture of the true intercessor at work. She said, "I will not let you go until you come and touch my son and bring him back to life." (2 Kings 4:30.)

After Elisha heard her plea, he first sent Gehazi, his servant, to the woman's house. Then Gehazi, taking Elisha's staff, went ahead and entered the room where the dead child had been lain. He touched the child, but the Bible says the boy's body did not move.

If you'll read in the next chapter, you'll know why the boy didn't move. The servant, Gehazi, was a man of a covetous heart. Naaman the leper offered Elisha great gifts for healing him of his leprosy. When Elisha refused the gifts, Gehazi said, "My master won't take it, but I will." Therefore, because Gehazi was greedy, he received the leprosy that had been taken from Naaman. (2 Kings 5:20-27.)

God knew Gehazi's heart; Gehazi had no power to give life to another person. But Elisha did because he was pure in heart. And when Elisha came to the widow's home, he breathed life back into that child and raised him up by the power of God.

First John 5:16 says, "If any man see his brother sin a sin which is not unto death, he shall ask, and he shall give him life for them that sin not unto death. There is a sin unto death: I do not say that he shall pray for it."

This is the true ministry of a priest who knows how to enter into the presence of God. The priest-intercessor enters into the fires of hell and breaks the power of those flames over his brother, and God brings and gives that brother life.

There are many people who have fallen away from God but have not sinned unto death. There are very few who have ever sinned the sin unto death. First John 5:16 shows us that the believer, when acting in a priestly authority, has the power and the authority to enter into the kingdom of Satan and say, "This child belongs to God. Let him go!"

God will honor your word, and He will give life to your loved ones through the mighty name of Jesus Christ, the Son of the living God. Hallelujah!

DO YOUR OWN "HOMEWORK"

I use to be foolish enough to try to do other people's "homework." For example, I thought I had to take everybody else's burdens upon me. After I had been doing this for a while, the Holy Spirit wised me up. He said, *Let them do their own homework.* Furthermore, He told me, *When you have done all that you know how to do in your own strength, then I will take your requests.*

Every believer has a responsibility to pray for his or her own needs. That is different than praying for a sinner. Sinners can't pray with any authority for anyone else. That is the believer's job. But each believer must pray for his own burdens, and not allow himself to become mentally overwhelmed by the burdens of others.

Don't limit your thinking by assuming that only one individual in a certain place is the answer to what you need. Listen to what the Holy Spirit told me about this. He said, *No, this is a great network.*

As you pray, the Holy Spirit, who is the Great Intercessor, will take up the cry, much like a huge switchboard. An incoming "call" may come in for intercession for your request and be transferred by God to, say, Australia. Then, once the need is felt in Australia, a believer who is on duty and whose heart is tuned in can take up intercession. In this way, God, through the

Holy Spirit, causes people to pray for your requests even when they do not know for whom they are interceding.

Do not only look to local help all the time. The universal church is the network we're talking about. So instead of getting your eyes fixed on just one person, get your eyes on Jesus, and He will delegate the prayer burdens as needed.

DON'T WATCH PEOPLE DIE AROUND YOU— INTERCEDE FOR THEM

When I answered the call on my life to go into deep intercession, God quickened my heart with Matthew 27:36, which describes the crowds of people who were sitting around Jesus and watching Him die on the cross.

After I read that Scripture, God told me, *If you want to see churches, nations, and individuals lose My touch of the Holy Spirit, then just sit down and watch them die.* I responded by exclaiming, "Oh, no, God! I couldn't stand to do that." So I began to give myself to intercessory prayer in the same spirit as Rachel, who cried, "Give me children, or else I die" (Gen. 30:1). And I have been praying like that ever since.

INTERCEDE OR BE SWALLOWED UP

The life of Jonah presents another clear picture of true intercession in the Bible. It shows how prayer can literally prevent the judgment of God. You know the story: Jonah was on a ship to Tarshish, running away from the call of God, when a storm blew up. The storm became so great that even the veteran mariners of the sea became fearful:

> **Then the mariners were afraid, and cried every man unto his god, and cast forth the wares that were in the ship into the sea, to lighten it of them. But Jonah was gone down into the sides of the ship; and he lay, and was fast asleep.**
>
> **Jonah 1:5**

Jonah was the only one in that ship who had any knowledge of the true God. So the shipmaster came to Jonah and entreated him to call upon the true God so that they might not perish. (Jonah 1:6.)

This is a picture of America today! We are in the midst of a terrific storm in the spirit. The hounds of hell are gnawing at the very throat of this nation. Therefore, I say to America, *Awake! Call on your God as never before. For the hour is late. There are many things that the church has yet to accomplish. She has yet to show forth the supernatural light of heaven. This nation was born to be a light to all the other nations of the earth. Don't let this light go out before its hour. You are the salt of the earth. You are the light of the world!* (Matt. 5:13,14.) *You hold in your hand the keys to the destiny of the world. Know that if you do not use them, as Esther of old was told, you cannot think that you will not suffer loss as well as your people.* (Esth. 4:13.)

This is the Holy Spirit's cry this hour to our nation. America is the last great bastion of freedom. We can't take it for granted that the beacon light of the Statue of Liberty will always be held high. It may not, if the church in America sleeps. However, we have the power through intercession to stop the judgment of God!

Jonah finally became willing to do God's work after his experience in the fish's belly. He went on to Nineveh, that great Assyrian city, and preached to them.

And Jonah began to enter into the city a day's journey, and he cried, and said, Yet forty days, and Nineveh shall be overthrown. So the people of Nineveh believed God, and proclaimed a fast, and put on sackcloth, from the greatest of them even to the least of them. For word came unto the king of Nineveh, and he arose from his

throne, and he laid his robe from him, and covered him with sackcloth, and sat in ashes.

And he caused it to be proclaimed and published through Nineveh by the decree of the king and his nobles, saying, Let neither man nor beast, herd nor flock, taste anything: let them not feed, nor drink water: but let man and beast be covered with sackcloth, and cry mightily unto God: yea, let them turn every one from his evil way, and from the violence that is in their hands. Who can tell if God will turn and repent, and turn away from his fierce anger, that we perish not?

And God saw their works, that they turned from their evil way; and God repented of the evil, that he had said that he would do unto them; and he did it not.

Jonah 3:4-10

By the power of intercession, you can turn the tide of judgment from a nation, from a church, from lives of individuals, from sons and daughters, and from husbands and wives. It is prayer that holds back judgment from all these. The intercession of hell is still crying out, *Give me that individual!* But you can hold hell back and bring heaven's light to earth and to your brother's door.

CHAPTER NINE

THE UNITY OF PRAYER AND THE SPIRIT

The closer I become to God, the more I realize how little I really know about Him. But that is not a bad thing. I don't have to know everything about God to love Him.

After all, I don't have to know all the elements contained in water to be able to drink it, do I? Do you know how to take the elements of water apart? Probably not! You don't have to understand something completely to enjoy it.

But that is what the church has been trying to do with prayer. These days, we have been trying to turn prayer and the move of God into a spiritual formula. We want it all down in black and white like a favorite recipe we can cook up the same way every time. And we become angry when we follow the "spiritual formula" and the results are not the same every time. But they are not supposed to be!

God is a God of unity, but He is also a God of diversity, not monotony. Sometimes we forget and try to put Him into the mold of a monotonous god. But we shouldn't do that. If we want to do the same things every time we come together to pray, prayer will become monotonous and boredom will set in.

If God continually did things the same way time and time again, eternity would be long, drawn out, and very boring, wouldn't it? But we know that is not the case. Eternity in heaven will be so exciting, thrilling, rewarding, fulfilling, and full of love, joy, and peace that we can't even fathom it. Hallelujah!

When you receive eternal life through Jesus Christ, you don't just endure the passing of time until you get to heaven. Sometimes you may get into certain church services that are so dull you feel you must pray for the grace to endure them, but God isn't like that church service! He is not boring. He is so exciting and so creative that eternal life could never be boring. Eternal life is not a duration of time; it is a quality of life that begins with the new birth and stretches into eternity.

Receiving eternal life is about growing in grace and in the knowledge of our Lord and Savior, Jesus Christ. This quality of life begins to so manifest itself within us that we inspire others. Soon others will begin to hunger and thirst after this eternal life.

YOUR PRAYERS BECOME A MEMORIAL IN THE PRESENCE OF GOD

Praying to God is one of the most marvelous, most beautiful, and highest privileges of spiritual life. It is also one of the highest exercises for the spirit.

Let's look in the Bible to see just how powerful prayer can be. Acts 10:1 recounts the divine visitation Cornelius the centurion received.

> **There was a certain man in Caesarea called Cornelius, a centurion of the band called the Italian band, a devout man, and one that feared God with all his house, which gave much alms to the people, and prayed to God always. He saw in a vision evidently about the ninth hour of the**

**day an angel of God coming in to him, and
saying unto him, Cornelius.**

Acts 10:1-3

An angel of God appeared to Cornelius and called
him by his first name. Isn't that wonderful? The Lord
knows you and me by name! This tells me that God is
acquainted with each one of His children, for He is the
God of the individual.

Let's continue looking at Cornelius's vision:

> **And when** [Cornelius] **looked on** [the angel of
> God]**, he was afraid, and said, What is it, Lord?
> And he said unto him, Thy prayers and thine
> alms are come up for a memorial before God.**

Acts 10:4

What did the angel mean by saying, "Your prayers
and your alms have come up before God as a
memorial"? The angel was saying that Cornelius's
prayers had entered the very court of God. Moreover, he
had been received there and recognized in heaven.

Intercession brings us into the very court of God,
where Jesus is. Because we're in Christ, anywhere He is,
we are as well. That means when He went back to the
right hand of the Father, we were taken back there too.
(Acts 2:33,34; Eph. 2:5,6.)

Therefore, when I'm praying, my spirit is just as glorified as my body will eventually be after the resurrection. My spirit can travel through the heavens and enter into the courts of God, where it can be seen and known.

So in Acts 10, God was telling Cornelius that his prayers had entered into heaven, where they had been recognized. Cornelius himself was known as a regular visitor there because of his prayers. He had been coming there daily in the spirit, and the Father had seen him.

In the spiritual realm, there is no distance. That is why Jesus can now carry on His work on earth by the power of the Holy Spirit, the indwelling Spirit of life within us.

Jesus said, "I'm going away, but I'm coming back." He said, "I will leave you, so I can come back to you." (John 14:28.) That may sound like quite a paradox, but it isn't. He disappeared, but He will return.

Cornelius was praying daily in reverence, holding God in such high esteem and honor that he was known in heaven. And God in His grace responded, "I recognize you because you have been praying, and I recognize that you need something. I will meet your need." (Acts 10:4.)

What was Cornelius's need? God ordained Cornelius to be the man who would break down the wall separating the Gentiles from the gospel. So Cornelius needed an opportunity to witness to the Gentiles. And because Cornelius was a man of prayer who had been crying out for God to visit his people, the Romans, God honored Cornelius.

God said, *I see this man Cornelius. My attention is focused on him, and I want to tell him that help is on the way.*

You know the story. In the evening, Cornelius went to visit another man of prayer who had gone up to a housetop to pray.

God brought two praying people together. The other man, Peter, went up to the housetop to pray and fell under the power of the Spirit. The Holy Spirit showed Peter that he would be involved in answering Cornelius's prayer. (Acts 10:9-48.)

Intercession is not only making appearances in the courts of heaven and being recognized there; it is also prevailing power to get needs met. When intercession is used with the name of Jesus, mighty power is made available. God honors Jesus' name. God moves in power when we use the name of Jesus.

PRAYER LIKE A RIVER

The gospel spread all across the ancient world through prayer. It spread to Philippi because of the prayers of a group of women who worked near a river. (Acts 16:13.) These women went to the river and prayed there, washing and cleaning as they prayed.

God heard and answered their prayers by sending Paul a vision of a Macedonian man who was pleading with him to "come and help." (Acts 16:9.) Paul did come to Philippi and found praying women by the riverside. He was able to spread the gospel and fulfill the prayers of the women by the river.

The river is a picture of intercession. Intercession flows from the hearts of men and women out to dry lands. But it doesn't only flow one way. When you intercede, you not only speak to God, but God also gives you something in return. Your prayers bring answers!

Intercession isn't about just sitting in a chair and pounding your fists. No! You pray by the power and might of the Holy Spirit, not your own. You have to enter God's presence through the spirit, not the flesh.

Now, it is true that you may have to break through some spiritual barriers to enter God's presence. Satan will oppose you because he doesn't want you to get into God's presence.

Satan tried to keep Jesus from reaching the throne of God. But Jesus made it through the spiritual barriers. He didn't make it to the throne just because He was born the Son of God. God didn't give Him any special favors. Rather, Jesus won the right to sit on that throne. He had to do some things to earn that right. He had to pass through this life without sin. Then He had to take on our sins and defeat the devil. Jesus paid the price to be seated at the right hand of the Father.

Jesus became more than a conqueror for our sakes Hallelujah! He earned the position of King of kings. He earned His position in the kingdom of God, and He can also bring us in. That is how your rank and position in the kingdom became established. He brought you into the kingdom to qualify you for God's many blessings. And He prepared the way for you and me to inherit eternal life.

THE SPIRIT BEHIND A PRAYER MUST MATCH THE SPIRIT OF JESUS

When Jesus came to earth, many of His own people, the Jews, couldn't recognize Him for who He really was. Many of them greatly revered God, but they never really knew Him. And when God became man in the body of Jesus Christ, many Jews could not recognize Him. (John 1:14.)

Before the incarnation, the name *Jehovah* was so powerful that many of God's people believed that all they had to do was say His name and fire would fall and destroy their enemies.

Actually, some of us today are guilty of the same error. We need to know that when we use the name of Jesus, the Spirit and the name have to agree. A passage from Luke illustrates this point:

> **And it came to pass, when the time was come that he should be received up, he stedfastly set his face to go to Jerusalem, and sent messengers before his face: and they went, and entered into a village of the Samaritans, to make ready for him. And they did not receive him, because his face was as though he would go to Jerusalem.**
>
> **Luke 9:51-53**

Many Samaritans resented the Jews because the Jews thought Jerusalem was the only holy city, and most Jews disliked the Samaritans as well. There was a rivalry between these two groups of people.

The Samaritans in Jesus' day didn't want to receive Jesus. And because of that, the disciples wanted to rain down judgment upon them. But that form of judgment was a practice of the old covenant. Jesus, the Mediator of the new covenant, came to bring peace. (Heb. 12:24.) Unfortunately, the Jewish people couldn't recognize Jesus' true ministry because they had expected something else. They wanted their Messiah to destroy their physical enemies. They wanted to call fire down upon them in revenge, instead of spreading the gospel of peace.

The Lord did not call us to division; He called us to peace. And eventually He will rebuke Christians for disputes such as these. Our spirits should line up with the name of Christ, which we bear. And we can't separate the name of Jesus from the Holy Spirit because they are one. We must unite in peace to see the work of God manifest among us.

I was born again many years ago in the old-time Pentecostal movement, but I didn't resent people from other denominations. Instead, the Lord told me to help people in other denominations come into the fullness of the Holy Spirit. But some of those old-time Pentecostals just couldn't believe that God would want outsiders coming into the fullness of the Holy Spirit. But God did.

Sometimes Jesus' disciples remind me of those people I knew who didn't want to bring others into the fullness of the Spirit. James and John, for example, asked Jesus, "Lord, wilt thou that we command fire to come down from heaven, and consume them?" (Luke 9:54). But we need to baptize people with fire, not consume them with it!

INTERCESSORS MUST HAVE A RIGHT SPIRIT BEFORE THE LORD

Even today we sometimes secretly take satisfaction from seeing someone who doesn't believe as we do being judged by God. When we see people, for example, who don't quite live up to our standards or dress quite the way we do, we often judge them. And when God's judgment falls on them, we may self-righteously think they deserve it. But the truth is that if it weren't for Christ's sacrifice, we all would deserve it. Each one of us is saved by *grace*. (Eph. 2:8.)

If we harbor an attitude of pride toward others, Jesus will approach us today as He approached His disciples in Luke 9:55: "But he turned, and rebuked them, and said, Ye know not what manner of spirit ye are of."

If you want to be a true intercessor—one who reverently enters into the presence of God by the name of Jesus—then your spirit must be humble. You must have an attitude that God can honor.

Practicing godliness doesn't stop at being born again. We must walk in love and cultivate a Spirit-filled life, consistently drawing from the Holy Spirit. Being godly is not something we do only once; it is a lifestyle we follow by continually keeping ourselves filled with the power of the Holy Spirit. (Eph. 5:18.)

Because of the Holy Spirit, God will always hear our prayers. Jesus said, "I thank You, Father, that You hear Me always." (John 11:41.) Did you know that when the Holy Spirit prompts your spirit to pray and you obey, God *always* hears your prayers? When you enter God's presence by the power of the Holy Spirit, you're sure to be heard and answered.

So, you see, prayer is easy! Praying to God should be as natural as speaking to a friend. Friends converse with one another. Jesus calls us "friends." (John 15:13.) How well do we know Him?

Jesus knows us; and we know Jesus, not just by head knowledge of the Word, but by spending time praying and talking to Him as a friend. Don't misunderstand me. I love the Word. I read it, devour it, and dwell in it. Yet, as I read through the Bible, many times I just fall on my face and cry, "Oh, God! I want to know You!"

WAIT ON THE LORD; MOVE WITH THE SPIRIT

You are not just spewing out words when you pray. Prayer is contact, communion, contact with the almighty God. As you come before the Lord in intercessory prayer, you learn that God has feelings. You learn to come into His presence as if you are an assistant to a doctor. It is as if you have worked with Him so long that you know exactly what He wants and what instrument to have ready for Him. In fact, you may get to know God so well that you can discern what He wants without His having to say a word to you. That is what it is like when you have spent enough time with the Master.

Do you remember Mary and Martha, Lazarus' sisters? Martha was encumbered all the time. She was busy and full of worries, when she should have been quiet. (Luke 10:40.)

Sometimes we do the same thing Martha did. Sometimes we overwork ourselves when, instead, we should simply be communing with God. The life of Christ comes from within, not from performing outward works.

Mary rested at Jesus' feet and listened to His words of life. And Jesus said, "Mary hath chosen that good part, which shall not be taken away from her" (v. 42).

Jesus says the same thing to us when we come into His presence. We do have to work, but when we spend quality time with God, we choose the better, eternal way. As we begin to intercede, we open our spirits to listen to the Holy Spirit.

The Bible says, "Wait on the Lord" (Ps. 27:14). That means we must be patient. We can't just rush into God's presence haphazardly. If we did that, hoping to stoke up a move of the Spirit, we would be like King Saul, who impatiently wanted to get his sacrifice over with, without waiting for the prophet Samuel to lead him into genuine worship.

As intercessors, we must wait as the Holy Spirit begins to direct our prayers. We don't always know how to pray as we ought. Thank God the Holy Spirit comes to our rescue! If I relied on my own natural mind and the power of my flesh to pray, my prayers would be very limited.

A REVOLT DIFFUSED THROUGH PRAYER

In the mid 1970s, a group of radical Native Americans went to Bartlesville, Oklahoma, to incite another Wounded Knee armed standoff. But our intercessory prayer group was on hand to pray for peace instead of war.

Our group met and began to pray as this situation developed. The Spirit of God began to pray through us until we almost sounded like participants in an Indian war dance. The tempo of our intercession was like the beating of war drums. All the others in the prayer group fell in together with me, and we began to join in the same language and the same voice. But then all of a sudden the tone of our prayers changed completely through the direction of the Holy Spirit.

Suddenly we dropped into the most peaceful and calm prayers in the Spirit. When the smoke of the spiritual battle began to clear, such peace came over us. I even saw a vision of men smoking a peace pipe. God told us, *In three days they will be moved out of here. The enemy's whole plan will fall apart.* He even said, *You'll read about it in the paper.*

Sure enough, in the newspaper I later read that the leader of the group had said, "We're disbanding, and we're getting out of here. We're gone."

As intercessors, we work together with God. God doesn't want to harm or destroy anyone; but in order to save His people, He won't hesitate to thwart the plans of the enemy. That is why it's best to be on God's side of the battle!

The following is a prophecy that God gave me about the times ahead:

I, the Lord, see and hear many of the long-range plans that are going on in the councils of men, as they gather together in this hour to do business for Me.

You must listen very intensely, very keenly to the voice of your God, rather than to the many voices that would seek to influence you to go in the wrong direction.

Guard very closely these gatherings together. It is becoming very fashionable to come up with such big plans of your own doing. But My plans are the best plans for My children.

Until there is a guarding of My plans, you will miss your personal and individual plans entirely.

Yes, I am still the God of the individual. I still deal one-on-one with My people.

Much as you network across the country and around the world through the telephone, so it is with the Holy Spirit and prayer. Your communication with Me links you with that person I will show you, so that your prayers go far beyond the stars above and into the throne room of the God of the ages. For I am the Ancient of Days, the Master Planner, the Designer of the universe. And if you will allow Me, I will let you enter into the high level secrets of God.

I will bar many who claim to understand scientific approaches to these secrets. I will close the door in their faces. But if you will come with Me into the secret council rooms of the Most High and close the door to the enemy, I will unveil before you My plans, purposes, intentions, and desires. I will show you My wisdom, counsel, and know-how. I will show you the inner workings of that life that you say you have within you.

I will truly open the tongues of My people. The Holy Spirit of God will be so strong upon you that you will stand in awe. You will see that God does display the brilliancy of His sons and daughters before the eyes of mankind. And there will even be days when you will almost be too dazed to speak.

So stricken and smitten will you be with My presence that the burdens and cares of this life will all suddenly lift from you in a moment—in the twinkling of an eye.

And you will be lifted and enlightened by the glory of the ages that are yet to come. You shall truly begin to taste of that which the Holy Spirit spoke of.

These are powers that are yet to be unveiled to you. For the powers of the ages to come are just on the verge of being tapped into by men.

For I have brought you to this point. I have trained and schooled you in past days, but I will now take you into a new era of the Spirit.

You will not be assaulted by the advancements of the devil. For I will suddenly equip and qualify you to withstand these advancements. And I will call the minds of all peoples back to the God who created them.

Men and women of the earth have felt they were so sharp in the business world, but I will add a dimension of the Spirit for My people who have the nature of My Spirit. They will be enlightened above the sons and daughters of this world.

I will lead men to riches in the earth and in the spirit that have been hidden for an hour such as this. I will show certain chosen ones the ways and means of transacting business both in the natural and in the spirit.

You will hear a word in season, focused by the Holy Spirit to enlighten your hearts and minds to a dimension that it has never yet known. But I purposed and planned it, even before I brought mankind into being. And I will fulfill this new dimension before My people who arrive in My presence.

I believe this word of the Lord is for this hour! God's people need to understand that we're entering a new day in the Spirit. God will open up the eyes of His people's understanding. (Eph. 1:18.)

The things of the Spirit are a part of the quality of life that is eternal. We will partake of this quality of life as God unveils it to us in the days to come.

Sometimes our finite minds are so wed to the world's system that God must completely sever that tie in order to join us to the life of Jesus Christ. As He does, we will be open to new levels of communion with God and His children through the art of intercession and prayer.

PRAY UNTIL THE FRUITS OF YOUR LABOR RIPEN

The staying power of prayer is one of the hardest things to maintain. Time is the great tester: That is why God is letting it roll on. Time will test the church of the living God.

When we first began our intercessory prayer meetings, we had a crowd of people who attended. But as the years rolled on, more and more people stopped coming.

As time went on, we saw our ranks diminish. But there were seven of us who stayed together for nineteen years. Hallelujah!

That requires God's help. You can't pray together for nineteen years without God behind you. All through those years, I counted it the greatest privilege and honor to pray with those seven warriors in the Spirit.

You may have to lay down some things in your life to become a great intercessor for God, but it is worth it. I'd rather lose many other things than that beautiful anointing of the living God from my life. All the sacrifices I have made have been worth it to gain such a precious, intimate relationship with God.

There have been times when God said, *Don't touch anything but Me. Leave everything else alone.* And He moved me on. After many years of deep intercession, God called me to teach and speak publicly again.

Those years of deep intercession for my loved ones and the lost, for great nations and intimate communities, for leaders and laypeople alike were some of the best years of my life. It is truly marvelous to see the fruits of my labor mature, bearing praise unto God. I have seen such beautiful and rich rewards for the work I have done in the Spirit. But most of all, I have been blessed to be able to do the work of the Lord for which one day I pray He will say, *Well done, my good and faithful servant.*

From Jazz Singer to Intercessor—The Life of Jeanne Wilkerson

Late in life, Jeanne Wilkerson was described by Kenneth Hagin Sr. as a "prophetess." She simply preferred to be called a "handmaiden of the Lord." "Prayer warrior" was another apt description of this five-foot, two-inch fireball grandmother, who spoke with a commanding voice under the anointing of the Holy Spirit.

Jeanne's beginnings, however, suggested a very different charted course in life. Jeanne was born on November 22, 1912, in the mining town of Granby, Missouri, in the foothills of the Ozark Mountains. Her parents, Thomas and Annie Courtney, enjoyed singing, and they cultivated this talent in their daughter. At age four, Jeanne took to the stage and began singing.

Jeanne's only sibling was her older brother, Thomas. The two remained close throughout their lives. Their father, Thomas, was the general manager of Granby's hardware store, which helped supply the mining company in town. Her mother, Annie, was an accomplished horse rider. The Courtneys attended the local Church of Christ, but Jeanne did not know about heaven, hell, or the saving work of Jesus.

Tragedy struck the family when Annie, Jeanne's mother, died in 1916, when Jeanne was only four years of age. To make up for her mother's absence, her father showered her with attention. She was certainly a daddy's girl.

Throughout her childhood, Jeanne continued to sing from the stage and was considered to be a child prodigy as she belted out the blues from her small frame.

Her father, Thomas, ate some type of impure food that caused serious ongoing damage to his liver. He fought the illness for a month in the latter part of the summer of 1922. Sadly, Thomas died just before medicine that had been dispatched from another town reached him. Jeanne, at age nine, and her older brother, Thomas, were orphaned.

Jeanne's father had been a member of the Odd
Fellows organization. He had made arrangements that in
the event of his death, Jeanne and Thomas would be
educated in the organization's boarding school in
Kansas City. So for the next six years, until Jeanne
turned sixteen, she was raised in the boarding school.
She developed her singing voice and her love for jazz
music. Jeanne was also a cheerleader for the football
team. She even won a "Charleston" dancing contest.
While in Kansas City, she also developed a love for the
movies of that era. When she was not on the dance
floor, she was in the movie theater.

Jeanne excelled in academics as well. She was
moved up two grade levels and graduated from high
school at age sixteen. After high school, she attended
and graduated from a Kansas City business school for
women. She then moved to Sapulpa, Oklahoma, to live
with her aunt and uncle. Jeanne got a job as a church
secretary for a church in Sapulpa.

Throughout her ministry, Jeanne mentioned how
much she hated boring and dead religion. Her time
working as a church secretary definitely shaped that
outlook. Jeanne typed up the pastor's sermons—and
was bored out of her mind when the pastor read them
back to her. She said the sermons seemed like "death
sentences." She used to laugh and tell the pastor, "I'll

type your sermons for you and come and listen on Sunday morning. But I won't be there on Sunday night, because I'll be out on the dance floor, where there is life." The love of her life was dancing, and "the Charleston" to her was the ultimate personal expression of that love.

Unbeknownst to Jeanne, things would take a radical turn in her life. One day she visited the home of a girlfriend who lived in Tulsa, a short distance from Sapulpa. While in Tulsa, Jeanne caught the eye of a young man, D.B. "Red" Wilkerson, as he was called back then. D.B. had been visiting the home of his brother, Bert, and his new sister-in-law. He noticed that Jeanne was across the street at her friend's house. Consequently, D.B. bribed his new sister-in-law to set up a date with Jeanne for him. It worked, and soon Jeanne and D.B. were "going steady."

D.B. had come to Tulsa as the Great Depression had started. He worked as an oil and lube man for a car dealership. He was a hard worker but didn't seem to fit the profile Jeanne wanted in a husband. She had said she would never marry a man who could not dance, but that is exactly what happened on May 17, 1930.

Jeanne's relatives were opposed to her marriage, saying D.B. was "an appleknocker and ridgerunner," in other words, a hillbilly from Arkansas. But they were married anyhow, and the couple moved into a modest servant's quarters apartment above a residential garage.

Neither D.B. nor Jeanne lived for the Lord early in their marriage. However, back in D.B.'s hometown of Fort Smith, Arkansas, his Pentecostal mother, Mary Wilkerson, prayed for the newlyweds. A few years earlier she had scraped together twelve dollars from the family grocery fund to give to her third son, D.B., so that he could hitch a ride to Tulsa to find work. She learned by mail that D.B. had married.

Mary Wilkerson began to correspond with her newest daughter-in-law, whom she had never met. Mary wrote, asking if D.B. and Jeanne were going to church anywhere. Jeanne wrote back, "No, we are not. It is too hot to go to church!" (This was in the early 1930s when air conditioning was not installed in very many places.)

Mary wrote back and answered Jeanne with these unforgettable words: "If you think it is hot now, where you are going [hell], there are no electric fans and no ice water." That shocked Jeanne because she did not even know that hell existed. Mary continued to encourage Jeanne and D.B. to go to church.

The couple was already struggling to make ends meet when they found out Jeanne was pregnant with their first child. The couple could not afford to live together and save for the expense of the delivery of the baby. D.B. had two jobs. He lubricated cars in the day and also worked evenings operating a parking lot that served events taking place in the old Tulsa Coliseum. It became necessary for Jeanne to go and live with D.B.'s parents in Fort Smith. This was not Jeanne's choice.

As Jeanne rode to meet her in-laws, she could see the meeting place in the distance. Although she did not frequently smoke, on this occasion she took out a cigarette and lit it. She wanted to present an air of sophistication to these "simple" Arkansas in-laws. When she met her new mother-in-law, Jeanne made sure she blew some smoke in Mary's direction. But that did not matter to Mary; she embraced Jeanne. Years later, Jeanne recounted that Mary "loved me into the kingdom of God."

In May 1931, D.B. and Jeanne's baby boy arrived. Jeanne nicknamed him "Tinker" because he was always so busy with his hands. The name stuck, and throughout his life he would be known as Tink Wilkerson.

Each time the Wilkerson family went to their old-time Pentecostal church, they asked Jeanne to come; but she resisted. On Sundays she preferred to stay home and prepare lunch. She knew she was empty and needed the Lord, but she was too proud to commit her life to Jesus.

One Sunday Jeanne relented and accompanied the family to church. She slipped into the back row for the service. As she sat in this church, Jeanne felt something different from the deadness she had experienced in other churches she had attended. She felt love from these church people. And there was a new emotion that came on her.

For the first time in her life, she felt aware that she was a sinner who needed God's forgiveness. Jeanne felt the strong conviction of the Holy Spirit. When the church service was over, she looked for the nearest exit. She felt she had to either run out of the church or run to the altar. This time she ran out the door. But like the old saying goes, "You can run, but you can't hide." Jeanne could run but she could not hide from the Holy Spirit's wooing. After this service, she no longer wanted to go out with a wild new girlfriend she had met in Fort Smith. She felt a new fear, a great unease about how she was living her life.

Jeanne's mother-in-law, Mary (known as "Mama" Wilkerson to her family), contracted a skin condition that produced sores on her body. One day the elders of the church came to pray for Mary at the Wilkerson's home. This peaked Jeanne's interest. She had never seen anyone pray for another person to be healed. Not wanting to be present when the elders prayed for Mary but wanting to see what went on, Jeanne hid behind a door and watched. The men laid hands on and prayed for Mary. The Spirit of God fell upon Mary, and she began to dance and spin around like a top! Jeanne knew enough about dancing to know that a lady at Mary's age (her mid-fifties) could not move like that by her own natural skill. Jeanne was fascinated by what she had witnessed, but she was even more surprised as the sores on Mary's skin rapidly cleared up in the following days.

Not too long after Mama Wilkerson was healed, Jeanne relented to her family's persuasion and went to church again. She had been running from God for about one year. Again, she sat at the back of the church. Again, she felt the magnetic force of the Holy Spirit leading her to Jesus. After the sermon, some people from the church approached Jeanne and asked, "Wouldn't you love to know Jesus?" When they said that, the dam of resistance broke and Jeanne began to weep. She asked Jesus to become the Lord of her life.

Moments later, people at the altar cried out, "Receive the Holy Spirit." Jeanne had no idea what they were talking about. Nevertheless, she said, "God, give me all You have!" Suddenly she began to speak in a foreign language she did not recognize. The words flowed out of her. Jeanne was experiencing the baptism of the Holy Spirit with the evidence of speaking in tongues. Jeanne's whole world had instantly changed.

From that day forward, Jeanne wanted all that God had to give. She vowed to pursue Him with the same vigor as she had pursued dancing and the ways of the world. Not long after her conversion, she was able to go back to Tulsa with Tink and reunite with D.B.

Life in Tulsa would not be the same. Jeanne did go back to see a movie, in which her favorite actress, Joan Crawford, starred. *Joan does not look the same,* Jeanne thought. *What's happened to Joan Crawford? She has changed.* The movies no longer appealed to Jeanne the way they once had. In truth, *Jeanne* herself had changed.

Jeanne's side of the family was shocked to find she had become a part of the Pentecostal movement. Pentecostals were often viewed by others as poor, uneducated "holy rollers."

While Jeanne visited her relatives in Sapulpa, the family managed to arrange a visit from her old church ministers. They attempted to explain to Jeanne why her Pentecostal experience was heretical. They must have been surprised to see Jeanne's enthusiasm about the things of God.

Although Jeanne did not yet know the scriptural authority to support the baptism of the Holy Spirit, she prayed and asked the Lord for the words to speak while the ministers tried to tear down her faith. Suddenly, she heard the words come out of her spirit, saying, "Go ahead! Pour your cold water on my fire. But in the end, my fire will heat your cold water!" The ministers could think of no rebuttal and left. Jeanne's family didn't think her faith would last, but they could not have been more mistaken.

Eagerly following her mother-in-law's admonition, Jeanne took her son and husband to the Full Gospel Tabernacle Assembly of God church in Tulsa. It was one of the first Pentecostal churches in Oklahoma and was commonly referred to in Pentecostal circles only by its street address, "Fifth and Peoria." Later the church was renamed Central Assembly of Tulsa. The Wilkerson family attended church there for the next forty-seven years.

Shortly after Jeanne began to attend the Assembly of God church in 1933, she decided to go to a prayer meeting in someone's home. Being such a new Christian, Jeanne had no idea what went on at such meetings. When she arrived, the house was full. And although people were all around, she felt alone, sitting by herself among strangers.

However, the feeling didn't last long. All of a sudden, Jeanne heard and felt a great rush of wind sweep through the house. It knocked her out of the chair onto the floor. She was "slain in the Spirit." And while lying on her back on the floor, she prophesied for over an hour. After that day, God cultivated a prophetic ministry in Jeanne.

Experiencing the supernatural, however, did not divert Jeanne from her earthly duties as a wife and mother. She was an immaculate housekeeper, always keeping her house in neat and tidy order. She was always investing herself in her growing family.

In October 1937, D.B. and Jeanne had their first daughter, Marilyn. D.B. had begun selling used cars and was able to provide a more comfortable living for his family. Jeanne was there supporting her husband and earnestly praying for him all the while. It seemed the right people always came across D.B.'s path at the right time, which opened further business opportunities. Looking back, D.B. knew his prospering business was due to the blessing of God showered down because of Jeanne's prayers.

Jeanne pursued the knowledge of God's Word with the same passion as she had danced on the dance floor. The Lord revealed to her that she had to pursue Him, because otherwise she would return to the pursuits of the world and her former life, which had so mesmerized her. Therefore, she attended seminars where she heard the teachings of old-time Pentecostal powerhouse ministers, such as Howard Carter, Smith Wigglesworth, P.C. "Daddy" Nelson, J.W. Follette and Raymond Richie.

After receiving all the wonderful teaching from these masters, Jeanne started her own ministry by teaching a college-and-career Sunday school class. She also led her own children to the Lord at an early age. Jeanne did not believe it was up to someone else to lead her children to Christ.

The Wilkersons were blessed with the arrival of their second daughter, Dianne, in 1942. Jeanne continued to teach in Sunday school. When World War II came, auto manufacturers stopped making new cars, creating a national shortage of automobiles. D.B. had to find used cars to sell so his infant business, which had gotten them through the depression, would survive. He had to scramble across the country to find quality used cars to sell to large oil companies in Tulsa needing fleets of autos. D.B. found favor with people who had a pipeline to good used cars in the Northeast. But finding the right cars was only half of the battle; getting the cars transported to Tulsa, Oklahoma, from around the country during wartime was another. Needless to say, there was a lot of "red tape" to cut through. And of course, Jeanne was praying. That could be the only explanation for D.B.'s ability to meet the right people with cars to sell and a method of getting them back to Oklahoma.

During the World War II years, D.B. literally searched the country to find cars and bring them back to Tulsa. He spent many nights away from the family. During that time, Jeanne kept the family in church and reared the children. She was able to balance her growth-in the Lord with meeting her family's needs.

After World War II, D.B. was able to purchase a DeSoto-Plymouth automobile franchise and establish his first car dealership in Tulsa. He would continue to sell cars in Tulsa for the next fifty years. Jeanne said that the more God blessed them financially, the more she humbled herself and sought God in prayer. She also knew God would multiply back all the money the couple gave in tithes and offerings. Through the years, the Wilkersons personally supported missionaries, church work, and Youth for Christ. D.B. and Jeanne realized that their growing business was also to be used to channel resources for spreading the gospel.

In the mid-1950s, D.B. acquired a Chevrolet franchise and let his older brother, Bert, and son, Tink, operate the DeSoto-Plymouth dealership. Jeanne began to teach a popular young married people's Sunday school class at her church. Jeanne also taught Bible study classes for people in mainline denominational churches who wanted to know about the fullness of the baptism of the Holy Spirit. She was quite content in this ministry. Her own three children had also grown, and she was a grandmother to Tink's two daughters.

But God had bigger plans for this little Sunday school teacher with a booming voice. His call was not for a wider ranging public ministry. Instead, God wanted her to go into private intercessory prayer. The year was 1961. When Jeanne was in prayer, she heard the Holy Spirit say, *Daughter, would you mind doing something for Me?* Jeanne responded, "Oh no, Father, what would You have me to do?"

God said, *Emergency hours are coming on the world, and I want many areas to be prepared for this time. I need intercessors who will stand in the gap and make up a hedge that is so lacking in the church.* God went on to tell Jeanne that in order to fulfill this role, she would have to leave all public ministry and devote herself to prayer. She did not know that, at the time she answered the call to intercession, the Cuban Missile Crisis, the

Vietnam War, and the charismatic renewal were just around the corner.

Jeanne obeyed and gave up the Sunday school class and the Bible studies. For five years she poured herself into intensive intercession. During this time of seclusion in prayer, the Holy Spirit taught Jeanne the art of intercession.

Jeanne started a Monday night prayer group. God told the small prayer group that they would cross international datelines. This befuddled Jeanne, and she thought, *Oh, God, how will I cross an international dateline from down in the church basement, where we meet?* God let her know that, because of the group's intercession, Christian satellite television would be introduced and cross datelines. Jeanne did not even know what a satellite was. But later in 1961, they learned that the first Christian television broadcast by satellite was beamed to earth.

About the same time that God called Jeanne into full-time intercession, she gave a prophetic word in her home church that was greatly misunderstood by some of the church members there. She received a good amount of criticism, which hurt her deeply. Consequently, Jeanne decided she would not prophesy in public again because of this wounding experience. She told the Lord,

"Father, if someone who does not know me does not cross my path and give me a word that I was acting in the Spirit on that occasion, I will not minister by prophetic word again."

Two years passed, but in the fall of 1963 Jeanne saw an advertisement that said a little-known Bible teacher was coming to Tulsa for a series of Full Gospel Businessmen's Meetings. Jeanne had never heard of him, but the Lord instructed her to go to the man's meeting, saying, *This man is a prophet. He will have a word for you.*

In obedience, Jeanne and D.B. went to the meeting to hear the man, Kenneth Hagin Sr., preach. At one point, Hagin stopped his sermon and pointed Jeanne out from the crowd, saying, "Sister, come up here." Brother Hagin proceeded to give a word of knowledge, which repeated exactly what Jeanne had prophesied two years earlier. He said God would vindicate Jeanne in spite of the controversy at her church. Brother Hagin then asked Jeanne to release a prophetic word to the congregation from the Holy Spirit.

Believing in the Scripture that says, "In the mouth of two or three witnesses every word may be established" (Matt. 18:16), Jeanne asked the Lord to confirm the prophetic word spoken by Brother Hagin. Not too long

after receiving Brother Hagin's word, Jeanne received a
telephone call from a group sponsoring a meeting
where a charismatic Roman Catholic, apostolic priest
would be ministering. On her way out the door to her
regular prayer meeting, the Lord told her not to go. He
said, *I want you to go to the other meeting. This apostolic
priest will have a word for you.*

Jeanne went to the large house where the meeting
took place and found it to be very crowded. As the
priest was ministering, he pointed at her and said,
"Sister, you are to minister to a certain man in this
place tonight." Jeanne did not move. She thought,
Well, I'm not the only one here who has a ministry. She
did not believe she should rush out just because
someone said there was to be ministry in the Spirit.
Jeanne thought she should wait and see if it was
someone else's turn to minister.

However, the priest was persistent. He said, "Sister,
you don't wear glasses all of the time, but you have
them on tonight. I want you to minister." Jeanne looked
around and saw that the woman sitting next to her was
wearing glasses. Jeanne thought, *Oh, it must be her the
priest wants to minister.*

Jeanne dismissed the call to minister again. The
priest could wait no longer and walked down the aisle

toward Jeanne. He opened his mouth in rebuke to her unresponsiveness, but he stopped short. He said, "I am stopped in my rebuke. Instead, the Spirit is rebuking me." He continued, "Your spirit has been deeply wounded, and you have taken much rebuke and been the subject of much misunderstanding."

The priest proceeded to recount the word Jeanne had given at her church and how she had been hurt by the subsequent fallout. "God will vindicate you," the priest said. Jeanne thanked the priest and went to minister to the other man at the meeting. Afterward, when Jeanne sat down, she prayed, "Thank You, Lord, but I must ask for a third confirmation." She had been so hurt by the experience that she felt she needed a double portion of confirmation by the Holy Spirit.

Later she went to another meeting where she did not know the speaker. Again, the speaker pointed her out and, in like manner, reviewed the recent past events, telling Jeanne that God would vindicate her.

After the third confirmation, Jeanne said, "God, that's it. I accept it." But God threw in a fourth confirmation for good measure. A woman in California called her and related a vision in which she saw all the rejection Jeanne had experienced. This fourth confirmation proved God would vindicate Jeanne.

With this assurance, Jeanne chose to continue to intercede, not becoming involved in any public ministry for six years. Looking back, she said those years were the most productive of her ministry. "I wouldn't take all the wealth in the universe for those years," she said. "Like Mary in the Bible, I sat at Jesus' feet really learning of Him." (Luke 10:39.)

One of the things she prayed about during this time was the Vietnam War. It came close to home in 1965, when she learned that a boy who had years before grown up in her church had been shot down and taken prisoner in North Vietnam. She constantly uplifted Lieutenant Colonel Robinson Risner in prayer during his brutal captivity. Risner was one of the senior ranking officers to lead the resistance organization comprised of the prisoners of war in the "Hanoi Hilton." One chronicle of the sufferings of the POWs in North Vietnam observed that Risner "absorbed as much or more punishment between November 1965 and the summer of 1966 as many of the men would face during their [Prisoner of War] term."[1]

Back in Tulsa, while Jeanne was in intercession, God would reveal to her when Risner was being moved by his captors. The Holy Spirit would also alert Jeanne when Risner and his fellow prisoners were near their physical and emotional breaking points from the torture.

She would plead their case before the throne of grace. She would pray, "God, if those men can battle there and suffer, I am willing to give myself in battle here against the forces that retain those men as prisoners on enemy territory. They will be set free!"

In March 1973 Jeanne's prayers were answered late one night as Risner and his fellow prisoners stepped off the Air Force plane at Clark Air Force base in the Philippines as free men.

After six years the Lord released Jeanne to go back into public ministry, but she still preferred her role as an intercessor. In the early 1970s she led a Bible study with a group of ladies who attended Boston Avenue Methodist Church. As a result, a wave of the Holy Spirit revival overflowed into denominational churches in Tulsa.

Jeanne began experiencing chest pain in 1970. It was so severe that she could not breathe when she lay down to sleep. Her son, Tink, made an appointment for her to see a cardiologist. However, Jeanne told Tink, "I will only go to the doctor appointment if I am out by 12:30 P.M." She had a Bible study to teach, and she didn't want to miss it!

The doctor diagnosed Jeanne with a main artery blockage, which prevented blood from flowing to her brain. "Mrs. Wilkerson," the doctor said with concern, "I would like to put you in the hospital and do a vein transplant." Jeanne replied, "Doctor, that's a 'vain' thought! No, doctor, you'll see me again, and I'll be well." The doctor turned to D.B., who was also present, and said, "Man, you have an optimist on your hands."

Jeanne could not resist, "No, doctor, I'm not an optimist. I have faith in the Word of the living God!"

After the appointment, Jeanne went on and taught the class. But when she got home, exhausted from a lack of sleep, she sat in her chair again. Jeanne was close to the breaking point. That night she cried out to God: "Father, tonight, lay me on the heart of one of Your great intercessors somewhere in the world. I have fought this battle to the gates. Lay it on someone else to carry it through with me." Instantaneously, the Lord answered, *I have lain you on the heart of one of My choice intercessors who is a "charwoman" in London, England.*

Suddenly, Jeanne felt the obstruction in her chest move and softly burst. She was able to breathe while lying down. She slept soundly that night and very rarely experienced any breathing or blood circulation problems for the rest of her life.

Some months later Jeanne visited with the widow of the British Pentecostal evangelist, Howard Carter. She shared with Mrs. Carter that the Lord had called a "charwoman" in London to intercede for her healing. Jeanne had no idea what a charwoman was. But Mrs. Carter knew exactly who the intercessor was.

A "charwoman" in the British vernacular is a name for a maid or domestic servant. Mrs. Carter further confirmed that a great female intercessor was known in England as a charwoman.

Jeanne's ministry expanded in the 1970s. She became an annual speaker at the Christ for the Nations Institute in Dallas, Texas. Although she received many invitations to speak in various places, she preferred to go to small places that had not had much exposure to the dynamic flow of the Holy Spirit. In 1976, she made her only ministry trip out of the United States to Mexico City. Because of Mexican government regulations, unregistered Protestant congregations could not openly gather in public. Jeanne's services were held surreptitiously at a country club in Mexico City. Jeanne later recalled that she felt the greatest anointing there in Mexico.

Often when Jeanne traveled, her daughter Marilyn would accompany her. Marilyn would sing before Jeanne ministered. They became an effective mother-daughter team. It was important that, through singing and worship, the right atmosphere be created so the Spirit could move on the people. Billye Brim noted that when Marilyn sang, the anointing "that put Jeanne over the top" would fall upon that place.

Also in the 1970s, D.B.'s many years as a reputable automobile dealer were recognized when *Time* magazine awarded him its prestigious "Time Quality Dealer" commendation.

D.B. and Jeanne's son, Tink, himself an auto dealer, became general manager for Kathryn Kuhlman's ministry. Tink served Ms. Kuhlman until her death in 1976. Tink was also appointed to the Board of Regents of Oral Roberts University. He was highly involved with the efforts to build the university's medical complex, the City of Faith.

D.B. and Jeanne's family relationships flourished as well. She was close to both of her daughters. Although her daughter Dianne lived in Oklahoma City, the cost of long-distance phone calls did not prevent her from talking to Dianne every day. Her dedication to family included regular contact with each of her eight grandchildren. She was very interested in what was going on in their lives. Nothing, seemed too trivial to discuss with her. She was always willing to answer a question about the Bible. Jeanne liked to go with D.B. and Marilyn's family to college basketball games at Oral Roberts University.

In September 1976 on a Monday evening in the basement of the "Fifth and Peoria" church, Jeanne uttered one of her most famous and intriguing prophecies concerning the fifty states of the United States of America. (A composite of this prophecy is found in Appendix A.)

Part of that prophecy revealed that Oklahoma would be spiritually linked to the state of Oregon. Jeanne believed that part of the prophecy was fulfilled when she accepted an invitation to speak in that state not too long afterward. She spoke, not surprisingly, on intercessory prayer for a week at the church in Oregon. As the week progressed, the numbers of people attending the prayer meetings multiplied. At the last service, an older gentleman stood up and spoke, giving the most poignant description of Jeanne's ministry yet: "Sister, you're the hottest thing to hit since the church burned down!"

Jeanne loved to minister to people one-on-one. Many people throughout the years came to her home for counsel and prayer. Often, if they needed financial help, Jeanne would give them some cash to help then get back on their feet. In fact, twelve years after Jeanne passed away, a family member was cleaning Jeanne's desk and found $1200 in cash stashed deep in a drawer.

The cash was the remnant of the "blessing bank" Jeanne used to help her visitors.

In May 1980 Jeanne and D.B. celebrated their fiftieth wedding anniversary. Another turning point in Jeanne's ministry occurred in 1980, although it was not a comfortable experience.

In the previous decade there had been a decline in the attendance and spirituality at Jeanne's home church. She and her prayer group had earnestly prayed for years that the Lord would send a great revival to the church. The Lord had given Jeanne a vision of the great revival and miracles He had in store for the church if the congregation would accept the unhindered move of the Spirit. She had clung to this vision, which kept her at the church even as its numbers dwindled.

One Sunday morning in the summer of 1980, Jeanne gave another prophecy that stirred much controversy in the church. As a result, her prayer group was prohibited from meeting at the church, where they had assembled for nineteen years. To leave the church she had labored in forty-seven years and wept over was a heart-wrenching experience. But she knew the Lord had released her. And, although the decision to leave "Fifth and Peoria" was painful, God would turn the situation, around and use it as a launching pad for the greatest phase of Jeanne's public ministry.

Jeanne questioned God, "What about the promise of revival You had given me?" The Lord replied that her prayers over the years would not be wasted. To the church that received her, God would transfer the promise of an outpouring of revival. He would honor her request at the next church that Jeanne made her home. Also in the summer of 1980, Jeanne's ministry expanded when she began a citywide Bible study. Among those in attendance were Billye Brim and her daughters.

In the fall of 1980, Jeanne and D.B., their daughter Marilyn, their son-in-law Roger, and their family began to attend services at the Sheridan Christian Center in Tulsa. The young pastor, who moved in the Spirit with wisdom beyond his years, had rejuvenated the work at that church. His wife ministered in song with a great anointing. Billy Joe and Sharon Daugherty welcomed the Wilkersons to their church, not really knowing what to expect. But Jeanne felt directed of the Lord to let Billy Joe be her pastor and to support the Daugherty's ministry.

The people packed into the church building on North Sheridan to hear the Word. On Sundays Billy Joe preached four services. It was moving to Jeanne to see many people at every service come for salvation. There

were also testimonies of mighty healings. Jeanne saw
the miracles performed that she had previously seen in
visions that were to take place at "Fifth and Peoria."
Jeanne knew she had found a church home where the
pastor was open to a great move of the Holy Spirit.
Wisely, she waited over five years to reveal to Billy Joe
and Sharon God's promise to her that He would transfer
the promise of revival to the new church.

Jeanne's public ministry expanded to wider
audiences when she reached an age when many people
were well into retirement. Jeanne wondered at this point
in time why God had preserved her to the age of
seventy. The Lord answered, *I have preserved you to
help and undergird younger ministries.* She spoke on
intercession at Kenneth Hagin Sr.'s Prayer and Healing
School and appeared on his television program. Billy
Joe Daugherty asked Jeanne to minister periodically at
his new church, Victory Christian Center, exposing a
new group of people to her ministry.

In the early 1980s the Cold War tensions between
the United States and the Soviet Union mounted. The
leaders of the Kremlin tightened their iron grip over their
European satellite countries. Despite the repression of the
Soviet totalitarian leadership, the Lord revealed to Jeanne
that, in the time period before the Rapture of the church,
there would be religious freedom to preach the gospel in

Russia. Mercy would be extended to Russia before judgment. When Jeanne told people about this revelation, it seemed like a remote possibility. In February 1982 Jeanne prophesied in one of Kenneth Hagin's services at Rhema Bible Training Center that leaders of the Soviet Union leaders would "fall dead on the spot."

Later in September of the same year, Jeanne prophesied about the Soviet Union again in a Sunday morning Victory Christian Center service held at the Mabee Center at Oral Roberts University. She revealed that God would move on the leadership of the Soviet Union one more time, and if they would not respond, He would deal with them.

She said Billy Joe Daugherty would one day minister to the people of Russia. Not long after Jeanne's prophecy, in November 1982 Soviet leader Leonid Brezhnev died after ruling the Soviet Union for eighteen years.[2] Yuri Andropov, the man who headed the secret police, the KGB, succeeded him. By February 1984 Andropov joined Brezhnev in the grave.[3] Konstatin Chernenko, Brezhnev's protege, became the latest Soviet leader, but he did not last long. He died in March 1985.[4] A younger man rose to power: Mikhail Gorbachev, who gave the Russian people more freedom under a policy named "Glasnost." Eventually, the Russian people did receive more freedom to come out from the underground and worship God openly.

Just as Jeanne's public ministry was expanding, on April 20, 1984, she had a major setback that was one of the greatest challenges of her life. She slipped on some water that had splattered onto her kitchen floor from a boiling pot on her stove. When Jeanne fell, she crushed the kneecap of her left leg and was unable to walk. Since she was seventy-one years of age at the time, the injury was one that could cause permanent disability. However, Jeanne was not the type of person who could enjoy life confined by limited mobility.

She was taken to one of the finest orthopedic doctors in Tulsa. The doctor happened to be Jewish, and Jeanne, in spite of her physical condition, could not pass up the opportunity to share her faith with him.

The doctor told her that reconstructive surgery would have to be performed. The knee would have to be totally rebuilt using other bones from her body. Jeanne declined the surgery, saying, "No, doctor, I will trust the Lord. My God is also your God." The doctor responded, "But I haven't been very good, and He isn't very pleased with me."

"I keep your Passover all the time," Jeanne replied with her wit intact, although she was still in pain. "He is

pleased with me, so I will trust Him." The doctor gave
Jeanne twelve days to decide if surgery would be
performed, but her mind was already made up. She
would trust God.

Jeanne went back twelve days later and told the
doctor she would believe God for a miracle, so instead
of surgery, he put a cast on her leg. She was told she
would be in the cast six to eight weeks. The doctor said
he did not know if the knee would rebuild itself. Jeanne
was immobilized and had to rely on a wheelchair to get
around. It was very frustrating to this active lady to be
confined in such a way. She wore the cast for five weeks
before going to see an orthopedist. The doctor took an
X-ray of the knee, and, with the film in hand, he told his
assistants, "Get that cast off of her. This knee is
rebuilding itself!"

Jeanne wore a splint on her knee for three more
weeks and returned to the doctor. During this
appointment the doctor found that the knee had rebuilt
itself completely! She was ready to start walking. Jeanne
reached out and touched the doctor, saying, "God bless
you, doctor, for going along with me. Thank you for
your kindness. I thank God in your presence for what
you have done." The doctor, with tears in his eyes, said,
"Mrs. Wilkerson, I did not do that. Your God did that."

As she was leaving his office, Jeanne said, "Doctor, you'll be in my prayers. I won't forget you." He replied in jest, "Well, a sinner like me can certainly use it." The next instant, his tone changed: "But seriously, Mrs. Wilkerson, I would appreciate your prayers." Praise the Lord!

Jeanne would face pain-wrenching physical rehabilitation to stretch and reuse the muscles that had been idle. Trying to walk again caused the muscles in her back to spasm. The spasm tortured Jeanne with intense pain and affected the nerves connected with her stomach. She was unable to eat, and she lost nineteen pounds, a loss that sapped her strength. It was initially believed that Jeanne's heart was the cause of her ailments. A battery of tests were administered to test her heart by the same cardiologist whom she had seen in 1970, but her heart was found to be in perfect condition. The stress on her body was from her injury to the muscles in her leg.

Jeanne knew she was also fighting a spiritual battle. She knew the adversary was trying to destroy her. She was physically weak, and her personality changed such that she seemed frail in contrast to her normal vibrant personality. Her spirit, however, never quit.

One night while she was sitting in her living room praying and battling in the Spirit, the Lord gave her a unique illustration to show her that the "cavalry" was being sent to the rescue. On this occasion in prayer, she lost consciousness of her pain and looked out of her window to see an angelic white horse with a warrior angel riding on it patrolling her backyard. She was awed when the horse and its rider galloped through the wall and entered the living room. The Lord made it known to Jeanne that her visitors were warring angels who had been sent to recruit help for her battle. The horse, however, was her private mount reserved for her arrival in heaven.

Jeanne later found out that, on the day she saw her angelic visitors, friends associated with Kenneth Copeland ministries, who were visiting London, England, had interceded for her healing. Gradually, she was able to walk without pain and regained her appetite. Her spunk and energy also returned, causing Jeanne to be zestful again.

By the fall of 1985 Jeanne resumed her public ministry with an even greater anointing after her grueling experience. She believed she was to help prepare the church to be the glorious bride of Christ for Jesus' return. In November 1986 International Women's Ministries named Jeanne, "Woman of the Year."

Jeanne had one last battle to fight. In January 1987 she was diagnosed with cancer. Insidious pain racked her body, and she fought the fight of faith. But this time she wanted to go home to be with her great love, Jesus. On April 20, 1987, she stepped into eternity, where she could forever sit at the feet of the Master, whom she adored.

Kenneth Hagin Sr. shared a revelation he received from the Lord about Jeanne's homecoming in the eulogy he gave at Jeanne's memorial service. At the gates of heaven, he prophesied, she was given a conquering warrior's welcome. (Brother Hagin's full word is found in Appendix B.)

Sadly, Jeanne did not live to see the collapse of the Berlin Wall and the fall of Communism. Russia did lift its repression on religious worship. Its people were hungry and open to hear the gospel. In November 1991 Pastor Billy Joe and Sharon Daugherty led the first of many mission groups from Victory Christian Center into Russia. Jeanne's daughter Marilyn Olsson was a member of the first group that traveled into St. Petersburg to help harvest the ripe field of people longing for spiritual freedom in Jesus. Marilyn was able to witness with her own eyes the fulfillment of the incredible prophecy her mother had shared almost ten years earlier.

Only when we reach eternity will we see the full effects of Jeanne's ministry of prayer and her humble willingness to teach people to sit at the Master's feet and know Him for themselves.

JEANNE WILKERSON

Orphaned at the age of 10 and raised in a boarding school, Jeanne Wilkerson was considered a child prodigy for her gift of singing the jazzy blues of the 1920s, but her first love was dancing the Charleston. As a young woman in the early 1930s, Jeanne met and married her husband of over 50 years, D.B. Wilkerson. Her Pentecostal mother-in-law led Jeanne to Christ, and during the dark days of the depression, it was on His provision the Wilkersons relied for D.B.'s fledgling auto dealership. D.B. went on to own and manage the successful Wilkerson Chevrolet dealership for almost 40 years.

Jeanne's biblical teachings came under the guidance of Pentecostal powerhouse ministers, such as Smith Wigglesworth. The beginnings of her ministry focused on teaching the children and later progressed to a young adults' class. The hallmark of her ministry came in 1961 when the Holy Spirit impressed upon Jeanne that *emergency hours* were coming upon the world and the church had very few intercessors. She was unaware of the Cuban Missile Crisis, the Vietnam War, and a charismatic renewal waiting just around the corner.

Jeanne responded by withdrawing from public ministry and spending the next six years leading a prayer group in the church basement. It was during this time of seclusion that the Holy Spirit taught Jeanne the art of intercession. She went on to lead that group of intercessors for the next 20 years.

She emerged from that time of seclusion eager to resume public ministry, and spent the 1970s and 1980s leading citywide Bible studies with traditional denominational churches who hungered to learn more about the baptism of the Holy Spirit. This "handmaiden of the Lord," as she preferred to be called, was a favorite speaker at Victory Christian Center, Christ For The

Nations, and Rhema Bible Training Center. In November 1986 Jeanne was named International Women's Ministries' "Woman of the Year." Jeanne Wilkerson went home to be with the Lord on April 20, 1987.

D.B. was reunited with Jeanne when he passed away on February 26, 2001. The two left behind a family grateful for the Christian legacy forged by the loving partnership that was centered on Christ.

ABOUT THE EDITOR

Brent Olsson is the grandson of Jeanne Wilkerson. He is a trial attorney who practices law in Oklahoma City, Oklahoma. Brent's practice emphasizes civil rights and insurance law litigation. He speaks to groups about the Christian foundation for American law and liberty. He also speaks on issues defending the Christian faith.

Brent graduated from Oral Roberts University with a bachelor's degree in History. In 1988 he attained a juris doctor law degree from the University of Tulsa.

Brent and his wife, Jene', have two young boys, Aaron and Josiah.

APPENDIX A

INTRODUCTION TO THE PROPHECY OF THE FIFTY STATES

Jeanne Wilkerson gave dramatic prophecies that related to the United States and other nations. During a Sunday morning service at Victory Christian Center in the fall of 1982, Jeanne prophesied that God would move on the leadership of the Soviet Union one more time, and if they would not respond, He would deal with them. In November 1982 Soviet leader Leonid Brezhnev died, and his two successors followed in death soon after. The Holy Spirit revealed to Jeanne that before Jesus returned, there would be a period of religious freedom in Russia. Following are fragments of her prophecy concerning the "roll call of the fifty states" and how each state would stand in the end times.

BIBLICAL PRINCIPLES OF PROPHECY

Before I share with you the prophecy that was given to me in October 1998 and its significance to the body of Christ, I want to define what prophecy is.

According to *Vine's Complete Expository Dictionary of Old and New Testament Words*, the word *prophecy* is defined as, "the speaking forth of the mind and counsel of God."

Prophecy is not meant to be used as "fortune telling." Prophecy is not meant to be used by the (false) prophet to manipulate people into doing the will of another human being.

True prophecy is when a messenger or representative of God proclaims the will of God that cannot be known by or through natural means. The prophecy can have reference to the past, the present, or the future. (Also taken from *Vine's*.)

The purpose of prophecy is to encourage, to edify, and to comfort believers. Prophecy may be given to an individual person and may address a specific situation that pertains to that one person. Many times this kind of prophecy is given in private and is meant for the ears of the recipient only. Other times, it is meant to publicly encourage the believer. This happens frequently in prayer lines, or even while the messenger is delivering a sermon, he may stop, single out a person, and give a word to him or her.

Sometimes a prophecy is given to an unbeliever, and through that prophecy, the person is directed to God and is brought to a saving knowledge of Jesus Christ.

Prophecy may also be given to the body of Christ in general. These prophecies may be given publicly to a large audience, or may be given to an individual who then passes that word on to others. Again, whether given to an individual or to a greater number of people, the prophecy is to encourage, to edify, and to comfort.

Prophecy is to be taken very seriously and reverently, as it is a Word given under the unction of the Holy Spirit.

PROPHECY OF THE FIFTY STATES

For almost twenty years Jeanne Wilkerson led a prayer group that met each Monday evening in the basement of Central Assembly of God in Tulsa, Oklahoma. The church was also known in the old Pentecostal circles as "Fifth and Peoria."

In the fall of 1976, one of the prayer meetings went very late into the night. The Holy Spirit wanted the group to intercede against satanic activity that was taking place in the nation's capital, Washington D.C. After a long period of joint prayer, the Spirit of prophecy came upon Jeanne. As a reward for the group's tenacity in prayer to throw the designs of Satan, the Holy Spirit gave the group a revelation concerning God's plans for the United States. The Spirit revealed that Governor Jimmy Carter would be elected president, and that America would have one last great revival.

Unfortunately, no tape records were there to capture the prophetic word, but through the years of Jeanne's ministry, she would often reference the prophecy and share portions of it.

The following is a composite of the Prophecy of the Fifty States, taken from the various recorded times when Jeanne discussed it:

In the fall of 1976, the Spirit of the Lord came upon me. For forty minutes the Lord poured out a prophetic word concerning the fifty states. When the two major political parties nominate a presidential candidate at their conventions, they take a roll call of states to determine which candidate each state will support.

Likewise, God was having His own role call of states to see if the people in each state would cast their vote for Jesus. God would bless the states that spiritually answered in the affirmative for Jesus.

The United States would have a period of time that God would give her to accomplish His purpose on the earth. Even though she had departed from God's precepts in many ways, America still retained the knowledge of God in a great mass of her people, so He was still going to bless this country. His people would awaken to realize the power they had through intercession to God.

At her birth, America originated from thirteen colonies. Thirteen is the number of rebellion (Gen. 14:4), but it is also the number of divine atonement. It is not coincidental that America is now comprised of fifty states. Fifty is the number of Pentecost (Lev. 23:15-16). America

did not have fifty states until the end times. When she had
fifty states, America would send missionaries to take the
knowledge of the Holy Spirit throughout the world in the
end times. Many natural characteristics of the individual
states would reflect their spiritual condition.

It was in the divine plan that America's symbol for
her insignia is the eagle, for she has many characteristics
of the eagle. The eagle soars to great heights, and when
the eagle grows old, it goes into a high place in the
mountain. It then begins to beat its old beak away and
loses its old feathers. Though the eyes of the eagle have
grown dim, suddenly the eagle's sight is renewed.

In the same manner, America would go through a
season where spiritually she would grow old and appear
to be on the brink of death. But God would intervene
and revive American's spiritual vitality, like the eagle's
youth is renewed. America will soar spiritually again.

Louisiana and California were two states where Satan
sought to seat himself in great strongholds. It was not by
happenstance that the name of the state of California
begins with the letter "C." It is the "cult" capital of the
United States. It is an enclave for the widespread
accepted practice of homosexuality. But God in His
grace was going to move in California. The city of San
Francisco will have a mighty outpouring of the Holy
Spirit—one more time—and it will be her last call.

God said by the power of the Holy Spirit, He would pull many people out of the fire of homosexuality—which is a fire lit by Satan. "Many of My own sons and daughters are participants in this unholy fire. The Holy Spirit will bring believers out of the fire. Having been delivered, they in turn will go in and bring others out of that bondage."

In the beginning of time God knew where the borders of the states would be. He hid great natural resources within the boundaries of the states that would vote to honor Him. God mentioned among others, Arkansas, Oklahoma, and Texas as states that would vote more in the affirmative for Jesus Christ than in the negative. Oil and gas are not the greatest resources that were invested in Oklahoma and Texas.

The nations of the world would seek to tap into the spiritual resources of Oklahoma and Texas in the last days. God has hidden away in these states great natural resources to generate wealth for His people in the last days.

The last great revival of the last days will be financed by much of the wealth from Oklahoma and Texas. The city of Tulsa in the last days would become a spiritual feeder station for the United States. People would come, be fed, and go back to their ordained places on the earth with the gospel message. Tulsa would be a prominent city during the millennial reign of Christ because of the great prayer that had arisen through the years from the intercessors that have lived in that city.

APPENDIX B

KENNETH E. HAGIN, SR.

I met Sister Jeanne Wilkerson and her husband, D.B., back in the fall of 1963 in the course of an eight-week seminar where I was teaching on the baptism and the ministry of the Holy Spirit. We were holding our meetings at Sheridan Road Assembly in Tulsa, Oklahoma.

I had never met the Wilkersons prior to these meetings. Sister Wilkerson was a stranger, when in one of the meetings I sensed the spirit of God wanted to use her, so I said, "That woman right there, get up and give whatever you've got." She got up and prophesied and gave a word that certainly witnessed with my spirit.

Though Sister Wilkerson was small in stature, when the anointing would come on, her voice would ring out strong, and she would give a prophecy. Through the years when she attended my seminars and I sensed the Spirit was not completely finished with what He wanted to accomplish at the meeting, frequently He would prompt me to call on her. She would never say anything unless I said, "Sister Wilkerson, go ahead now and obey God." The prophecies she gave were relevant to the topic of the meeting and right on the mark.

CONTACT WITH GOD

She was a humble woman and was never pushy. Rather, Sister Wilkerson was the type of person who wanted to obey God and did not seek out to be heard or seen.

There is one prophecy Sister Wilkerson spoke to me that stands out in my mind. In the spring of 1968, she prophesied that in the fall of that year, I would have an experience similar to Enoch's in that he was caught away into heaven and I would receive a new revelation.

Six months later my only sister passed away. My wife and I had gone to Garland, Texas, to be with my sister at the time of her death. We returned to the house where we were staying late that night. As I was getting ready for bed, I began to think back when I was sixteen years old, growing up in McKinney, Texas, just twenty-five miles away.

My memory focused on August 23, 1933, when I knew I was dying. It was 106 degrees, but I was cold and they had hot water bottles around me to keep me warm. My heart did stop and my spirit ascended to where the top of the house was, when I heard what I believe to be Jesus' voice say, "Go back, go back, go back to the earth. You can't come yet; your work on earth is not done." I descended right back down in the room and back into my body. But while I was out of my body, I saw my mother bent over me holding my hand.

My thoughts shifted to my sister's passing. I knew that when she went up to heaven, she would have seen our family around her bed having great concern. Just as that thought entered my mind, I suddenly saw a beam of light about as big as an elevator on my bed. In an instant, I was caught up in that beam of light and went to heaven itself.

Next, I saw my sister, whose death I was just thinking about, talking to Jesus. Jesus saw me, he stopped talking, and my sister turned around and saw me. She said, "Ken, don't feel so bad that you couldn't pray the prayer of faith for me." She indicated there was a reason why, but didn't discuss it with me. My sister went on to describe all of our family members she had seen in heaven.

Then my sister made the statement that gave me the revelation that Sister Wilkerson prophesied I would have. My sister told me, "You see, people up here are not concerned about the natural. They're not interested in whether you got a new dress, a new car, or the amount of money in your bank account. But they know everything that happens spiritually." She asked me to talk to one of her sons that had backslidden away from the Lord. "I'll know when he makes his decision to surrender to the Lord." That son did eventually come to serve the Lord.

After my experience, I remembered the Scripture where Jesus said there is more rejoicing in heaven over one sinner that repents than over ninety-nine just persons. (Luke 15:7.)

On the afternoon of April 20, 1987, I was sitting at my desk signing diplomas for our students graduating from Rhema Bible Training Center, when the Spirit of the Lord told me that Sister Wilkerson was getting ready to go home to heaven on that day.

At Sister Wilkerson's memorial service, I felt impressed to share a word of prophecy that described the homecoming reception she received in heaven.

THE RECEPTION

Listen! 'Tis the morning hours in Glory.
A shadow through the mists doth now appear.
A troop of angels sweeping down in greeting.
A welcome home rings out with joyous cheer.

A traveler from the earth is now arriving,
A mighty welcome's ringing in the skies.
The trumpets of a host are now resounding,
A welcome to the life that never dies.

Who is the victor whom the angels welcome?
What mighty deeds of valor have been done?
What is the meaning of these shouts of triumph?
Why welcome this soul as a mighty one?

She is but a woman, frail and slight and tender,
No special mark of dignity she bears.
Only the Christ light from her face cloth glisten,
Only the white robe of a Saint she wears.

She is but a soul redeemed by the blood of Jesus.
Hers but a life of sacrifice and care.
Yet with her welcome all the heaven is ringing,
And on her brow a victor's crown she bears.

How came she thus from sin's benighting thraldom,
The grace and purity of heaven to obtain?
Only through Him who gave His life a ransom
Cleaning the soul from every spot and stain.

See! As you gaze upon her face so radiant,
'Tis but the beauty of her Lord you see;
Only the image of His life resplendent,
Only the minor of His life is she.

See with what signs of joy they bear her onward,
How that the heaven's ring with glad acclaim!
What is the shout they raise while soaring upward?
Welcome! Thrice welcome thou in Jesus' name!

Rest in the mansion by thy Lord prepared thee
Out of the loving deeds which thou has done,
Furnished through out by thoughts and acts which
     have portrayed me
Unto a lost world as their Christ alone.

CONTACT WITH GOD

Hear how thy lovely harp is ringing;
Touched are its strings with hands by thee unseen,
Know that the music of thine own creating,
Heaven's melodies in hearts where sin has been.

See how the atmosphere with love is laden,
And that with brightness all the landscape gleams.
Know 'tis the gladness and the joy of heaven
Shed now by rescued souls in radiant beams.

Oh, that here on earth we may learn the lesson
That Christ enthroned in our hearts while here,
Fits and prepares the soul for heaven,
Making us like Him both there and here.

Doing the simple and homely duties
Just as our Christ on the Earth has done.
Seeking alone that Christ's own beauty
In every heart should be caused to bloom.

Showing all men that the blood of Jesus
Cleanses all hearts from all sin below,
And that the life of Christ within us
Transforms the soul till as pure as snow.

When we thus to the dark, cold river,
No sin, no darkness, no death is there.
Only great joy that at last the Giver
Grants us anew of His life to share.

APPENDIX C

FREDA LINDSAY

Jeanne Wilkerson was a very unique person. She preached with tears and laughter all in one breath. Jeanne would stop every so often and prophesy, then start to sing in a high soprano voice in worship to the Lord. Our students at Christ For The Nations simply loved her. They entered into worship, a thousand of them, not just because someone asked them, but because Jeanne carried an atmosphere of loving God.

Some people think of women as the weaker sex, but Jeanne spoke with a real dynamism. There was nothing weak about Jeanne Wilkerson. She spoke with authority. The word I would say best described her preaching delivery was that she had "dominion." She didn't serve God in a rocking chair. You know, in Genesis the Lord said He wanted us to have dominion. People with dominion are not weak-kneed. They are bold. Jeanne was every bit that.

She was a tiny person, and yet she had such a big voice that always kind of surprised me. She knew the power of God and spoke with such an anointing. The minute she stood behind that pulpit, you knew she meant business and was in a battle. She always had a new, fresh message to impart to the students. From the moment she opened her mouth to the last "Amen," you knew you were in the presence of God.

I remember Jeanne saying that she sat at Jesus' feet for sixteen years getting to know God. That was her desire—her goal. That was the cry of her heart. She mentioned, "You know when God is in a service, it's not boring." I remember she also said, "Jesus had the greatest prayer life of any man, and yet He was King. Why would Jesus need to pray? He's the Son of God. Since He, in fact, took so much time to spend with His Father in communication, then it behooves us to make time to communicate with the Lord."

Jeanne was a very attractive lady, who always dressed beautifully and looked like a princess. I'm sure she could have been a model if she had chosen that career. I took note that Jeanne was a godly mother and a wonderful wife. She was a friend to everybody. I used to watch our students come up to her after she finished speaking; she would take time with everyone. There was no one too high or too low. She was just like a mother. Sometimes she would put her arms around them; sometimes I would see her praying with them, at other times counseling them. One minute you'd hear her laughing, and the next you'd see her shedding a few tears with them. She'd have a prophecy or pray in tongues over them. She saw a leader in every person that she met. She put a spark in every one of those young people. So, I'm sure that she left a great legacy here for those thousands of students that heard her speak, and that fruit will continue to grow until Jesus comes.

She had a word from God for everybody, and that is what made her special. She gave me a word of great encouragement in 1975, at a time when Christ For The Nations was under tremendous financial pressure. It was less than two years after my husband, Gordon, had died and the board elected me to head our ministry. We were building additions to the campus and had acquired apartments for housing, yet at that time we were in a struggle to make mortgage payments.

Jeanne admonished me to look to God as my source. God had raised this work up, and Gordon had laid a good foundation. She said, "Just know that God will take you through." It was just the thing that I needed, and the Lord brought it to pass just like she said.

We loved her dearly and will never forget her!

ENDNOTES

Chapter 1
1. Strong, "Greek," entry #335, p. 11.
2. Webster, p. 678.

Chapter 2
1. Christ For The Nations Newsletter. Dallas: Christ For The Nations, 1980s.
2. Ibid.
3. Ibid.
4. Ibid.
5. Ibid.
6. Ibid.
7. Ibid.
8. Ibid.
9. Webster, p. 282.

Chapter 3
1. Larkin, pp. 34,35.

Chapter 5
1. Strong, "Greek," entry #2200, p. 34.

Chapter 6
1. Webster, p. 665.
2. Ibid., p. 1542.

The Life of Jeanne Wilkerson
1. Rochester, pp. 161,162.
2. Isaacs, pp. 341,342.
3. Ibid., p. 351.
4. Ibid., p. 356.

REFERENCES

Isaacs, Jeremy and Taylor Downing. *Cold War on Illustrated History 1945-1991*. Little Brown and company, 1998.

Larkin, Clarence. *Dispensational Truth or God's Plan and Purpose in the Ages*. Philadelphia, Pennsylvania: Rev. Clarence Larkin's Estate, 1920.

Rochester, Stuart I., and Frederick Kiley. *Honor Bound American Prisoners of War in Southeast Asia 1961-1973*. Annapolis, Maryland: Naval Institute Press, 1999.

Strong, James. *The New Strong's Exhaustive Concordance of the Bible*. "Greek Dictionary of the New Testament. Nashville, TN: Thomas Nelson Publishers, 1990.

Webster's New World Dictionary of American English, Third College Edition. New York: Simon & Schuster, Inc., 1994.

For further information write:

Brent Olsson
P.O. Box 721396
Oklahoma City, OK
73172-1396

*Please include your prayer requests
and comments when you write.*

Additional copies of this book
are available from your local bookstore.

HARRISON HOUSE
Tulsa, Oklahoma 74153

PRAYER OF SALVATION

A born-again, committed relationship with God is the key to a victorious life. Jesus, the Son of God, laid down His life and rose again so that we could spend eternity with Him in heaven and experience His absolute best on earth. The Bible says, **"For God so loved the world, that he gave his only begotten Son, that whosoever believeth in him should not perish, but have everlasting life"** (John 3:16).

It is the will of God that everyone receive eternal salvation. The way to receive this salvation is to call upon the name of Jesus and confess Him as your Lord. The Bible says, **"That if thou shalt confess with thy mouth the Lord Jesus, and shalt believe in thine heart that God hath raised him from the dead, thou shalt be saved. For whosoever shall call upon the name of the Lord shall be saved"** (Romans 10:9-10,13).

Jesus has given salvation, healing, and countless benefits to all who call upon His name. These benefits can be yours if you receive Him into your heart by praying this prayer:

Heavenly Father, I come to You admitting that I am a sinner. Right now, I choose to turn away from sin, and I ask You to cleanse me of all unrighteousness. I believe that Your Son, Jesus, died on the cross to take away my sins. I also believe that He rose again from the dead so that I may be justified and made righteous through faith in Him. I call upon the name of Jesus Christ to be the Savior and Lord of my life. Jesus, I choose to follow You, and I ask that You fill me with the power of the Holy Spirit. I declare right now that I am a born-again child of God. I am free from sin and full of the righteousness of God. I am saved in Jesus' name, Amen.

If you have prayed this prayer to receive Jesus Christ as your Savior, or if this book has changed your life, we would like to hear from you. Please write us at:

Harrison House Publishers
P.O. Box 35035
Tulsa, Oklahoma 74153

You can also visit us on the web at
www.harrisonhouse.com

THE HARRISON HOUSE VISION

Proclaiming the truth and the power
Of the Gospel of Jesus Christ
With excellence;

Challenging Christians to
Live victoriously,
Grow spiritually,
Know God intimately.